Trout Streams
of Alberta

A Guide to the Best Fly-fishing

Jim McLennan

Illustrations by David Soltess

Johnson Gorman Publishers

The Publishers
Johnson Gorman Publishers
3669 – 41 Avenue Red Deer Alberta T4N 2X7 Canada

Credits
Cover photograph by Jim McLennan.
Author photo by Lynda McLennan.
Cover and text design by Full Court Press.
Printed and bound in Canada

Acknowledgments
Financial support provided by the Alberta Foundation for the Arts, a beneficiary of the Lottery Fund of the Government of Alberta.

COMMITTED TO THE DEVELOPMENT OF CULTURE AND THE ARTS

Canadian Cataloguing in Publication Data
McLennan, Jim, 1953–
Trout streams of Alberta
(Blue ribbon books)
ISBN 0-921835-17-5
1.Fly fishing–Alberta–Guidebooks. 2. Rivers–Alberta–Guidebooks.
Alberta–Guidebooks. I. Title. II. Series.
SH572.A4M34 1996 799.1'1'097123 C96-910131-7

5 4 3 2 1

Author's Acknowledgments

Many people provided assistance essential in the production of this book. Thanks first to Dennis Johnson of Johnson Gorman Publishers for resurrecting a project that was dying on the vine and to David Soltess for great illustrations and great patience each time I wanted to change something on one of the maps. Bob Scammell introduced me to Dennis Johnson and then provided photographs and information on the streams and fishing in the Peace country.

A large group of people provided information freely when I requested it and then read parts of the manuscript to correct or verify my interpretation of their information. They are Kevin Van Tighem, Garry Szabo, Bryan Kemper, Richard Brown, Martin Paetz, Jim Epp, Roman Scharabun, Darwin Monita, Dan Bell, Vic Bergman, Jim O'Neill, Carl Hunt, Ken Kohut and Dr. Darryl Smith.

In scanning this list, I note that these are also the people at the forefront of the on-going effort to protect and preserve Alberta's cold-water fisheries. It is not coincidence that the people with the information are the people with the influence.

Additional thanks go to Bill McMullen, Dr. Robert Behnke, Bruce Masterman, Jack Dennis and Glenn Smith for various assistance and to Gary Borger for writing the foreword.

Barry Mitchell was a strong supporter of this project and also provided information on the Red Deer, North Saskatchewan and Athabasca systems.

Lastly I must express my gratitude to my wife, Lynda, and my daughter, Deanna, for putting up with my disappearance into the basement for a year to write this book. We'll fish more next summer.

NOTE: *Chapter 13, "The Dream Season," appeared in the 1996 edition of* The Alberta Fishing Guide.

To two Bobs:

Scammell, for years of friendship and help, and for not mentioning the fact that he is more qualified to write this book than I am; and Paget, for the years of effort and gifts—recognized and anonymous—that he has given to Alberta's trout streams.

Contents

FOREWORD

THE GREAT SPINE of mountains pushing its way boldly through the thin skin of the western prairie, that range we call the Rockies, harbors the greatest trout fishery in the world. From the heated desert grasslands of its southern terminus to the frigid plains of reindeer moss at its northern end, this jumble of upthrust and broken mantle has birthed more streams than any one angler could hope to fish in a lifetime. There are sweeping rivers, tiny brooks, inviting streams, and vexingly challenging spring creeks, not to mention a host of lakes and ponds, each with its own character, its own fishes, its own set of problems to test the fly-fisher's skills.

Jim McLennan has spent his life exploring the water-rich boreal reaches of the vast domain. His home waters in the province of Alberta are the stuff of dreams for most other fly-fishers, and he has given himself devotedly to them. He has settled tiny dries on the glassine surface of the mighty Bow's mile-long flats to fool big browns and rainbows sipping delicately in the tricky currents. He has waded the rushing and intimate little Crowsnest, dropping a huge salmonfly imitation under overhanging conifers to lure the robust trout sheltering there. He has explored for scrappy cutthroat that rise eagerly to the fly in the jingling mountain brooks that splash out of snowfields high on the shoulders of the Rockies' most spectacularly rugged mountains. He has drifted streamers through the swift waters of the Oldman for its fiercely aggressive bull trout.

Many could undoubtedly make the same claim. But through it all, Jim has stopped to listen, to learn, to remember. You see, it's one thing to simply fish; it's a totally different thing to draw knowledge from the experiences that rivers teach. Knowledge can be synthesized into a better understanding of the fish, of their food organisms, of the ecosystems we love so well, and ultimately, of ourselves. It is Jim's purpose in this book to give that much sought knowledge.

Do not take it lightly, my friend, for Jim is a superb fly-fisher who writes from a deep understanding of all aspects of the sport. It's most satisfying to watch him cast and work a fish, a delight to follow the steps in his dressing of a delicate dry, and great fun to be with him as he rows the rivers and gives his insightful guidance about holding positions and the hatches and patterns to match them. This is not just another "where to fish" book. This is a book about *the fishing*. And it's a good one.

    –GARY BORGER
    WAUSAU, WISCONSIN

Part 1

Trout

*I*T WASN'T SO MANY YEARS AGO *that fly-fishers considered the state of Montana the ultimate western destination. And while Montana's status has not diminished, things are getting a little crowded at the top as the Canadian province of Alberta is now recognized as a sort of northward extension of Montana, but with fewer anglers.*

This recognition began with the "discovery" in the late 1970s of the wonderful trout fishing downstream of Calgary on the Bow River. The explorers, if you will, were Leigh Perkins, A.J. McClane, Lefty Kreh and Charles Brooks—well-known and well-traveled American fly-fishermen who pointed out to Albertans and the world the quality and value of that resource.

Now some of our other streams are being noticed—streams like the Crowsnest River, the North Ram and the North Raven. Not everyone is happy about this, for when fame descends upon a trout stream, solitude vanishes. I too regret the loss. Yet I believe we are fortunate to have famous streams that attract tourists, for this turns the economic wheels and convinces our policy-makers that trout in moving water are valuable. We are equally fortunate to have hundreds of streams throughout the province that will never be famous. The future of these streams is more secure because of the others' fame.

I hope that exploration and discovery will always be part of the fly-fishing experience in Alberta, and I smile at the thought that my grandchildren might cast flies on waters I will never see.

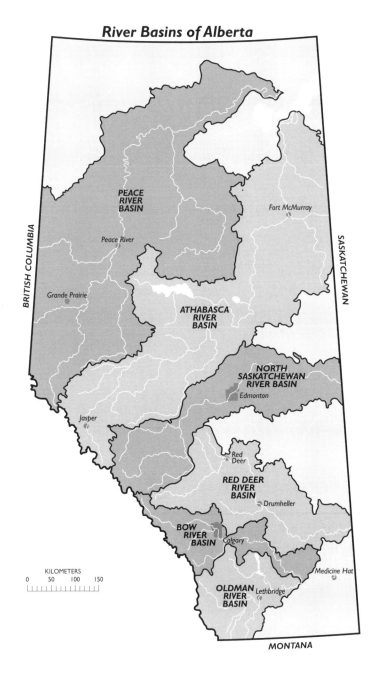

River Basins of Alberta

BRITISH COLUMBIA

SASKATCHEWAN

PEACE RIVER BASIN

Fort McMurray

Peace River

Grande Prairie

ATHABASCA RIVER BASIN

NORTH SASKATCHEWAN RIVER BASIN

Edmonton

Jasper

Red Deer

RED DEER RIVER BASIN

Drumheller

BOW RIVER BASIN

Calgary

Medicine Hat

KILOMETERS
0   50   100   150

OLDMAN RIVER BASIN   Lethbridge

MONTANA

≈ 13

I

The SEASONS *of* *a* TROUT STREAM

LATE ONE SPRING AFTERNOON the canopy of ice, softened by two weeks of March sunshine and weakened by the pull of current underneath it, groans, breaks and begins to move. By evening, huge, broken slabs of ice are drifting and colliding with one another, some tipping down to gouge pits in the gravel of the stream bed. In July many fish will find confidence and security in these new lies, but for now everything is chaos and confusion. To a creature tuned to sense the movement of a single minnow on the far side of the pool, the thunderous sounds of ice grinding on ice and gravel are terrifying. To the trout it is an earthquake in the midst of a hurricane, and their whole world is violently rearranged.

For some days the fish are stunned by the trauma of the breakup, and they stay in the deepest recesses of the river. But the direct sunlight that now pierces the water after four months' absence accelerates the tempo of all life in the stream. Through the winter the cold-blooded trout needed very little food, and a single leech or lethargic dace minnow would last them days, but now the warming water draws the trout out of the deep pools and into quicker, shallower water, where stream life thrives and food is more abundant.

It is now April and the nymphs of little Blue-winged Olives, the *Baetis* mayflies, are also reacting to the sunlight and beginning to stir in the gravelly riffles. They will be hatching into adult flies soon, and as they become more active the trout find them and begin to feed heavily. Success brings companionship, and soon each riffle has a group of trout working the nymphs boldly, as if to make up for lost time.

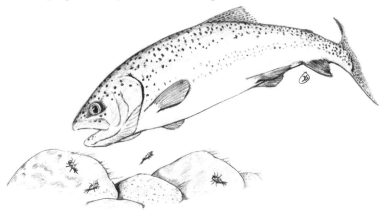

An angler who walks his dog along the river each day stops on a high bank to look down into the water. In the head of a pool he sees shadows gliding forward and back, side to side, appearing and disappearing. Occasionally there is a silver flash as the side of a bright rainbow trout catches the light. The angler carries no rod, yet he smiles at this gentle and certain signal that a season has turned.

As the days get longer the fish feed hard and put on weight quickly. But soon the mature rainbow trout, pushed by something stronger than hunger, begin to move upstream toward the big river's confluence with a small creek. They congregate in the pools immediately below the mouth and wait. When clouds cover the sun and rain increases the flow, the fish move into the creek. Over the next two weeks hundreds of rainbows, including some of the largest fish from the big river, move many miles up the small stream to find the right combination of depth, current speed, gravel size and water temperature to complete their mission.

From a bridge over the stream in a small town, a grade four science teacher points out the spawning fish to the children in her class.

When these fish are gone the brown trout in the main river continue their drive toward summer. More insects hatch—big, flopping March Brown mayflies and then hyperactive caddisflies. The caddis are always the first to draw fish to the surface, and the word quickly spreads through the fly shops and fishing clubs in town: "I saw fish rising in the flats today," or "There were some good ones eating caddis below the bridge this afternoon." The fish soon share the smooth glides with anxious anglers.

By mid-May the trout in the main river are in full summer mode. Gone and long forgotten are the darkness of winter and the uncertainty of early spring. But the trouts' dues are not yet fully paid. The warm days have been melting snow in the high country along the western spine of Alberta, and through ravines, coulees and creek beds the brown, ugly, necessary snowmelt from twenty-five weeks of winter is rolling eastward, churning and gathering debris from forest, field and mountain.

Eventually the brown water reaches the trout, and in a few days the stream becomes unrecognizable from above and below. The velocity of the current doubles, the volume of water quadruples and the fish are once again in shock. A few young trout and whitefish are taken by the fierce currents and die, but the mature fish—Nature's survivors—move to the edges of the stream where friction between earth and water slows the current. Some of these places were dry ground just a few days earlier. The fish pin themselves tight to the banks and the bottom, fins reaching and groping in a dark, rolling world.

Though runoff brings every conceivable bit of junk into the stream—leaves, branches, whole trees, mud and litter—it also carries things for the fish to eat. Earthworms, beetles, ants and spiders wash in with the high water, and the fish soon adapt. So much food arrives with the dirty water that many fish actually gain weight during runoff.

Runoff lasts until mid-June, and with receding water the spawned rainbows return—thin, bruised and tired but eager to feed. As the water clears and drops, the trout once again spread out through the river. The biggest fish claim the best lies, where food, shelter and relief from current are all present. Smaller fish find places of safety but must move daily to feed.

Through July the water warms, plants grow on the stream bottom and insect activity increases. It's summertime and the livin' is easy. Fish are jumpin' and the cottonwood fluff flies. Each midday delicate Pale Morning Dun mayflies emerge, and some fish feed on them, but in the evening the stream begins to hum with activity. Each night the water column becomes caddisfly soup as thousands of pupae swim toward the surface to emerge as adults. When the sun is off the water, the fish gorge on both emerging pupae and egg-laying adults. The trout might dine with a certain dignity on mayflies, but they pig-out shamelessly on caddis. They jump, chase and slash at the flies, sometimes coming completely out of the water, trying to catch a pupa before it reaches the surface and flies away. The mayhem continues for hours after the sun is gone, and through the night the fish feed boldly in water just a few inches deep, taking security in darkness rather than depth.

Yet the largest fish are often reluctant to feed on the surface, preferring to eat bigger things in safer places. There are always small fish around, juveniles that have not yet learned to fear their older relatives. There are also large insects on the bottom—two-inch stonefly nymphs among the big rocks in fast water and fat dragonfly nymphs in the slow, silty places.

In the heart of the summer, a hot, dry wind ripens the grain in the fields and blows grasshoppers into the water off the arid south-facing banks of the river. The fish are frightened by the first few hoppers that crash-land on top of them, but they quickly learn that the splat of a hopper means an easy meal. By mid-August the fish are moving to the prime hopper banks each afternoon in anticipation of the banquet.

In August the tributary delivers to the main river scores of yearling rainbow trout—six- and seven-inch fish that have spent their first year of life in the small stream. The little creek is no longer capable of providing the food they need, and on August evenings downstream of the mouth the small trout feed eagerly, their rise forms pocking the surface of the river like rain. Soon big browns and a few nasty bull trout discover the little fish and begin to cruise the flats each evening like sharks.

The changes brought to the river valley by autumn are confirmed by many human senses. The copper-colored grass that hides the hoppers is split by a coulee of blood-red willows, and the elegant cottonwoods brighten to brilliant yellow while the spruce withdraw to an ominous blue-green. Even the water seems bluer now, reaching almost indigo, reflecting a sky deepened by the sun's lower autumn track through it. The aromas carried by the September breeze are no longer lush, lazy and green, but sharp, focused and purposeful. Each day at sunset the valley fills with wingbeats and *haronks* as the Canada Geese gather and prepare to migrate.

The final major hatch of insects begins in September. It is

the autumn version of the Blue-winged Olive—the same *Baetis* mayflies that started the season will also finish it. The adults appear each afternoon for five weeks, and in early fall the fish feed on them through the afternoon and evening. By early October, though, the water has cooled and there is only a two-hour window each day when the fish acknowledge the tiny flies.

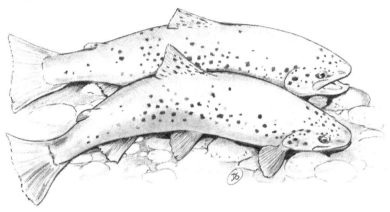

The trees are now barren of leaves, and a skim of ice forms along the slow edges of the river each morning. The rainbow trout are slowing down, but the big browns are anxious and restless. They move far up the river, like the rainbows in the spring, seeking the place ancient instinct tells them is right to spawn.

From a slate sky large flakes of snow fall straight down and dissolve in the cold, gray water while a dark male brown trout pairs with a butter yellow hen in the gravelly tailout below a log jam. They begin the dance. A ruffed grouse hunter, working the creek bottom with a Brittany spaniel, stops to watch this ritual of regeneration.

In the main river, the trout gather again in the slower, deeper pools—places well suited to the demands of winter, where they can expend little energy and use up their accumulated body weight slowly.

On Christmas Eve a man walks along the river with his dog and fourth-grade son. He stops, closes his eyes and begins to explain to his son life under the thick roof of ice.

2

The COLD-WATER FISH *of* ALBERTA

I N ALBERTA IN THE 1930S the daily limit on trout was fifteen and the possession limit was thirty. But the streams then weren't any more productive than they are now, and the population of wild fish gradually declined under the weight of such generous limits. No one worried too much though, because in those days it was standard practice to simply add fish from hatcheries whenever the numbers of wild fish seemed a little low. Often the hatchery fish were non-native species like brown, brook or rainbow trout.

Heavy stocking of hatchery trout was the main focus of provincial fisheries management for many years until someone came along with a better idea. The late Dr. R.B. Miller, a zoologist at the University of Alberta from 1939–1959, concluded a study in 1952 showing that the stocking of hatchery fish in streams already carrying a reproducing population of wild trout was a bad idea. He found that stocking caused overcrowding, increased competition and ultimately an overall *decrease* in trout population in the stream. I'm sure Dr. Miller raised some eyebrows when he first reported these findings to colleagues and government administrators, especially when he suggested that the way to improve the fishing was to stop stocking the streams. This was radically different advice from the usual thinking of the day, which said if you want more fish in the stream, pour some in.

But they must have listened because Alberta immediately stopped routinely stocking trout in moving water. History has since proved Dr. Miller correct, and this policy, combined with reduced catch limits in later years, has been a significant factor in the preservation of Alberta's stream fisheries. Though Alberta was one of the first jurisdictions to manage fisheries this way, later studies in Montana and elsewhere confirmed Dr. Miller's findings, and the policy of not stocking streams has been widely adopted by enlightened fisheries managers in other places.

The face of Alberta's trout stream fishing, however, had been changed forever by the random, helter-skelter stocking program that existed before Dr. Miller's findings came to light. The introduced species sometimes found a niche because of depleted populations of native fish, and in many streams the newcomers completely replaced the natives. Hindsight tells us this is regrettable because in many cases the native fish—usually cutthroat or bull trout—have never recovered and are now absent from much of their original range.

But time has also proved some of these introductions to be astute, even if only accidentally so. For example, though cutthroat and bull trout are the native fish of the Bow River, they have been almost completely replaced by rainbows and browns introduced early in the twentieth century. Some people resent this "takeover" by the new fish. However, we now know that it is unlikely the bulls and cutthroats would have survived the stresses brought upon the river by the city of Calgary in the way the more resilient rainbows and browns did. Without some of these introductions, stream fishing for trout might not exist in parts of Alberta today.

So Alberta's trout streams today carry a blend of native fish—primarily cutthroat and bull trout, mountain whitefish and arctic grayling—as well as introduced rainbow, brown and eastern brook trout. Though those from the latter group are not *native* to the waters where they now live, they are all *wild* individuals, having come from eggs spawned in the streams by their parents rather than from a hatchery. Thank you, Dr. Miller.

RAINBOW TROUT

I have no recollection of the first fish I caught, but chances are it was a rainbow, for there are more of them caught in Alberta than any other trout. Rainbows have been successfully introduced to many naturally barren lakes throughout the province, and they also thrive in many of our streams.

There are two kinds of wild rainbow trout in streams: those that are spawned in fresh water before going to the ocean to mature (called steelhead and renowned for their great strength) and those that spend their entire life in fresh water. From within the latter group are likewise two kinds of rainbow trout: those in the Bow River and those everywhere else. The Bow carries a hard, silver, powerful strain of fish, aptly described as Bow River bullets. I have caught rainbow trout in many parts of the world, but those downstream of Calgary run harder and jump higher and more often when hooked than any other trout I've found. When the late A.J. McClane, the celebrated angling author, fished the Bow with me in the late 1970s, he in fact compared their stamina, speed and strength with that of wild West Coast steelhead.

Mr. McClane's comparison may have been more astute

than we realized. According to Dr. Robert Behnke of Colorado State University, one of the world's leading trout taxonomists, the rainbows in the Bow River may indeed *be* steelhead. Dr. Behnke believes that while the rainbows used to stock the Bow came from diverse sources, most traced back to the first sources of hatchery rainbows, which were often steelhead from north-western American rivers like the McCloud and Rogue.

Though rainbow trout now inhabit every major Alberta river system, our only native rainbows are believed to be in the upper Athabasca River system. The earliest documentation is found in the journal of Dr. Walter Cheadle, where he describes a fish he found near Edson on a trip across Canada in 1863. In addition, employees of the Grand Trunk Pacific Railway noted rainbow trout near Hinton and Jasper in 1910–11, before record-ed fish stocking had begun. Scientists speculate that after the recession of the last Ice Age, Moose Lake, in the headwaters of the Fraser River system, may have been connected to the Miette River, which is a tributary of the Athabasca in Jasper Park. For a time rainbow trout may have had a clear path from the Fraser into the Miette before Mother Nature chose the current placement of the Continental Divide.

Populations of pure-strain natives are still thought to swim in the Freeman River in the Swan Hills area as well as Wampus Creek and a few other streams in the McLeod River system. Athabasca rainbows are a unique fish, a slow-growing, long-living species that can eke out an existence in the cold, harsh headwater streams, where even bull trout find it tough.

The province began stocking rainbows in both lakes and streams throughout Alberta in about 1939. Rainbows were chosen because they are easy to raise in hatcheries, they grow quickly if adequate food is available and their showy fighting style appeals to anglers.

One unfortunate characteristic of rainbow trout is their tendency to hybridize easily with native cutthroat trout. The rainbows dominate this game, and after relatively few generations of hybridization, the cutthroat characteristics tend to disappear, often completely. Consequently it is rare for the two fish to remain present and distinct in the same fishery for very long. Rainbow trout have thus taken over from native cutthroats in many areas of western North America, including Alberta.

While Alberta's best rainbow trout streams are undoubtedly the Bow and Crowsnest rivers, there is fine sport available in many other streams, from the quick Maligne in Jasper Park to the McLeod, the Oldman and the Waterton. And while a large part of me regrets the fact that the rainbow's success has often been at the native cutthroat's expense, I find it difficult to be disappointed when a Bow River rainbow delicately takes my Elk Hair Caddis at dark and then instantly empties my reel of backing. It is hard to imagine a better game fish for a fly rod than a rainbow trout. He is beautiful, fast, acrobatic, eager to feed on the surface and resilient enough to withstand most of what late twentieth-century civilization throws at him. What more is there?

BROWN TROUT

I've never caught a brown trout in a lake. It's not that they never live in lakes—it's just that I've come to associate them with moving water. And though they live in some huge rivers, to me brown trout will always belong in small streams. Brown trout have led me from Alberta's North Raven River to Pennsylvania's Letort Spring Run to New Zealand's sweet Mararoa Valley, and fishing for them is always like chasing shadows of the wind. They appear and disappear at will—abundant one day, less than vapor the next.

I like to fish alone for brown trout. Maybe it's because my most fragrant memories of brown trout involve a small cast of characters: them and me. I know people who never fish alone and that puzzles me. I also know that if I couldn't fish alone at least part of the time, I probably wouldn't fish at all. A psychologist could probably tell me what this means, but I'm not about to ask.

There is a section of stream that a friend showed to me in confidence many years ago. I've fished it once a season since then, always by myself. It is in many ways a peculiar piece of water with an abundance of riffles and a shortage of pools. The fish are brown trout, not particularly plentiful but occasionally big. Last year this creek was especially good to me one day in mid-May. I walked miles, as you must on this stream, and each time I found deeper water, I found brown trout. Some of them were rising to a sparse hatch of March Brown mayflies, and some of them took nymphs I drifted along the deep banks.

When I had gone upstream as far as I wanted, I sat down beside a pretty pool with my feet in the water. For a few minutes I lay back and pretended to have a nap, but mostly I stared at white clouds framed by the tops of spruce trees. Eventually I sat up and replaced my dry fly with a small streamer, then pulled a sandwich and an apple from my vest for lunch. I put the apple in my mouth and flipped the streamer into the pool. A brown trout grabbed the Woolly Bugger before I could grab the apple, so I played and landed the fish from a sitting position with an apple in my face and a sandwich in my lap. I noted that this wasn't exactly how they did it in those super-serious fishing videos and concluded that it was especially good to be alone this day. It's funny how some of the things we remember about fishing trips have nothing to do with fishing, yet at the same time they perfectly *define* fishing.

Brown trout are native to Europe and Asia, and were one of the fish (along with salmon and grayling) that the English nun Dame Juliana Berners had in mind when she wrote the first book about fly-fishing in the midfifteenth century. Their wide natural range, along with successful introductions on every continent except Antarctica, have made them the most common of the world's trout and chars.

Brown trout have been fished for since at least the third century A.D. and have developed a greater degree of wariness than our native North American trout and char, which have only been encountering anglers for the last couple of hundred years. This thousand-year head start has made today's brown trout a little harder to catch and a little more resistant to the increased fishing pressure of modern times. By contrast, our North American rainbow, cutthroat and bull trout are still very susceptible to predation from human anglers, and some populations have been completely decimated. But brown trout have had more practice and are more capable of surviving the human onslaught.

They also thrive in water of lower quality and higher temperature than other species of trout and char. As well, brown trout spawn in the fall, when conditions in the streams are most stable and predictable, and this gives them an advantage over the rainbows and cutthroats, which spawn in the spring when stream conditions are most volatile and unpredictable. Put simply, brown trout can take care of themselves, and this ability has stood the species in good stead for centuries in trout streams around the world.

Brown trout made their appearance in North America in 1883, when eighty thousand fertilized eggs were brought to New York State from streams in the Black Forest of Germany. Industry was booming and human population was growing in the northeast at the time, and the stocks of native eastern brook trout were shrinking. Once introduced, the hardier, more adaptable brown trout took hold, filling in the gaps, but they were not exactly greeted with open arms by the anglers of the day. Many resented the brown for what they perceived as its displacement and domination of their beloved brook trout. In truth the brook trout were already on the way down when the browns arrived. The choice was not, as the fishers believed, between brook trout and brown trout, but probably between brown trout and nothing. There also is some regret over the success of brown trout in Alberta, and though there were some differences here, in some of our waters the choices ultimately may have been similar.

Brown trout arrived in Alberta in 1924, when they were introduced to the Raven River and lakes in Jasper National Park. Though they have been absent from Jasper for many years, brown trout have done well in the Raven and other foothill streams of west central Alberta as well as in the Bow River between Banff and Arrowwood. They now form an important entry on our list of trout stream tenants.

The brown trout's need for cover and protection is met particularly well in the slow flows and undercut, brushy banks of streams like the North and South Raven rivers and numerous other tributaries to the Red Deer and North Saskatchewan rivers. Browns are shy and feed most actively in times of low or indirect sunlight—on cloudy days, at dawn and at dusk. They are also maddeningly temperamental, sometimes refusing to feed even when all factors seem to indicate they must.

As fly-fishing guru Ernest Schwiebert says, "There is almost nothing as lifeless as a brown trout river when its moody fish are strangely off their feed."

A big brown trout is like a proper English butler who moonlights as a pro wrestler—this morning inspecting a size 24 midge emerger with disdain, and tonight, after dark, body slamming a huge streamer right at an angler's feet. A brown trout is an enigma dressed in fins and scales.

Bull Trout

I haven't caught a lot of bull trout, but I remember my first one. It was in a tiny stream in Jasper Park that I used to like to fish as a kid, a nondescript little creek that runs chalky white in summer just like the big Athabasca into which it flows. It was easy to miss the creek where it tumbled off the rocky slope and through a culvert under the highway, but farther down on the floodplain it was more interesting, and I could usually expect to find a few small rainbows there.

One humid July evening I was fishing up a favorite grassy bank when not a rainbow but a small bull trout came up through the milky water and daintily sipped my dry fly. I dragged him in and released him with barely a second thought. All I knew of bull trout then was that they weren't supposed to take dry flies.

It would suit the story nicely to say that I've been a passionate bull trout aficionado ever since, but it just isn't true. Most of the bulls I've caught since then were taken accidentally when I was trying for other main-event fish like rainbows or cutthroats or brown trout.

Bull trout are a member of the char family and also used

to be called Dolly Vardens until taxonomists decided they are two different species and the ones in Alberta are bulls. Scientists also tell us that bull trout are native to "barren watersheds draining the glaciated interior of the western mountain region." Translation: Bull trout live in uniquely beautiful places, and you won't catch one unless you're in sparsely populated wild country—the kind we don't have much of anymore in the rest of North America.

The bull trout's native range includes every Alberta river system from the Oldman to the Peace. It is the top predator in the nutrient-poor headwaters, where the water is cold and the growing season brief. When you live in a neighborhood where food is scarce, you learn to grab whatever you can, whenever it is available. And bull trout do just that, feeding boldly and decisively when the chance comes, with little concern for the source of the food. Old-timers sometimes used live mice for bait.

Though their numbers are usually meager in the headwater streams, bull trout can grow big in small places if they're left alone. The boys with the mice caught ten-pounders in some pretty tiny creeks. Their large size made bull trout attractive to anglers, and their aggressive behavior made them easy to catch. If you concluded that a small population of large, hungry fish would be easy to overharvest, you'd be right. And that's exactly what happened through the middle third of this century. As more of Alberta's high country was opened up to the oil, gas, logging and mining industries, more people could get to more of the backcountry where bull trout live. And when they caught bull trout they took them home.

Loss of habitat and competition from introduced species of fish have also hurt bull trout in Alberta, as has the construction of numerous dams that block their seasonal migrations to feed and spawn. Early in the twentieth century the bull trout was Alberta's most common trout species, occupying streams from the headwaters to the prairie reaches. During my lifetime though, they have been reduced to novelty status in much of Alberta, little more than a sad reminder of what used to be.

In short, bull trout were headed for oblivion and in desperate need of help. It arrived, and none too soon, with the formation in 1993 of the Bull Trout Task Force, a coalition of conservation organizations, government agencies and scientists dedicated to aiding the recovery of the bull trout in Alberta waters. In 1995, in a burst of surprising good judgment, our elected representatives made the bull trout Alberta's provincial fish and simultaneously implemented protective regulations on its harvest. The regulation is simple: You can't kill a bull trout in Alberta, period. Nice work, guys.

Today southern Alberta's best bull trout fishing is probably in the upper Oldman River system, where some big bulls share the pools with small cutthroats, who have reason to be worried. A surprising number of bull trout are also being caught in the Crowsnest River below Lundbreck Falls. But the best bull trout fishing in the province, and some of the best on the continent, is in the Muskeg, Little Smoky and Kakwa rivers near Grande Cache.

I haven't caught a lot of bull trout, but I remember the last one. It was a warm summer day on the Oldman River and I was, as usual, fishing for something else. I hooked a small rainbow in a riffle, and as I dragged him back toward me a green ghost swooped out from under a rock ledge and took a run at my little fish. I cut back my leader, put on a big streamer and flopped it out, trying to make it behave like the panicky rainbow. On cue the bull trout made another swoop and took my streamer. I landed him, but this time before releasing him I made a point of pausing to think about and appreciate what had just happened.

With good fishing regulations now in place, we'll have the chance to catch more of these great native fish in the near future than we have in the recent past. I'm expecting a few ten-pounders in the coming "new good old days." And the first time I catch one of these prehistoric giants, when I'm cradling him in shaking hands, I'm going to try not to think of that fish itself, but rather of where his kind has been and what the presence of his kind means to a river.

CUTTHROAT TROUT

It's a long, rough logging road that takes you from the campground on the center fork of Prairie Creek, southwest of Rocky Mountain House, up past the swampy headwaters of the north fork and ultimately into the Ram River drainage. But it's a drive worth making, especially in the fall, when the sky is cloudless blue, the morning frost lingers until midday and the North Ram's big cutthroats want dry flies.

From its headwaters east of Abraham Lake, downstream to its confluence with the South Ram, the North Ram River's clear waters flow through a wide gravel floodplain cut into dense evergreen forest mixed with occasional aspen and willow. Deer, moose and elk live here, and the last time I fished it the warden told us there was a grizzly in the valley. The North fork of the Ram River may be Alberta's best cutthroat stream, and its story is a shining example of what can be accomplished through thoughtful, enlightened management.

The North Ram is a high elevation tributary to the North

Saskatchewan, so its water stays cold well into summer. It is subject to scouring in spring and anchor ice buildup in winter. The insect population is fair but not nearly as dense as that of very productive rivers like the Crowsnest or Bow.

There were no fish of any kind in the river until west-slope cutthroats from southeastern British Columbia were introduced in 1955. The North Ram was chosen for the introduction partly because it has a set of falls that keeps the cutthroats isolated from other species, particularly rainbow trout with their hybridizing ways.

The North Ram was a mediocre fishery producing small numbers of small fish until 1982, when the provincial government implemented full-time no-kill, no-bait regulations on the stream. This change has allowed the North Ram to develop into an exceptional fishery. Though the population is still relatively small, the fact that the fish can be caught more than once means that fewer of them can satisfy a larger number of anglers. The new regulations also allow the fish to get bigger and ensure there are adequate numbers of mature fish left to spawn each spring. Today the North Ram gives a capable angler a very real chance to catch twelve- to twenty-inch west-slope cutthroats in beautiful, wild surroundings.

Cutthroat trout are native to Alberta's Bow and Oldman river systems, and have been introduced to the Peace, Athabasca and North Saskatchewan systems. In many areas the purity of the cutthroat strain has been diluted by hybridization with rainbow trout. The hybrids, which often look like rainbows with faint cutthroat marks under their jaws, are quite common in many Alberta streams, including the Bow and lower Oldman rivers. Pure-strain cutthroats are rarer, but are still found in the Ram, some other tributaries to the North Saskatchewan, like the Bighorn River, and the streams of the upper Oldman system. They have recently been successfully introduced into a naturally barren part of the Torrens River in the Peace River drainage.

Cutthroat trout were made for dry flies, and this trait has endeared them to western fly-fishers for decades. Once the water temperature has reached about 50° F, you can expect to find them sticking their noses out of the water. When there is a good hatch in progress, cutthroats will rise to it. When there is no hatch in progress, they will probably rise to your dry fly anyway.

The cutthroat is proving to be an ideal candidate for catch-and-release management in Alberta because it is popular with anglers and is relatively easy to catch. In 1995 the provincial government implemented no-kill regulations on the Livingstone River, an upper tributary to the Oldman, and similar regulations are slated for the Torrens River in 1996. We are told to expect more no-kill regulations on other cutthroat streams in the future.

In my dreams it is permanently autumn on the high country creeks of the Ram River drainage, and what I notice first is always the colors—of the sky, of the river valleys, of the cutthroats and of the flies I use to catch them. And, dreaming or not, to watch a golden-flanked fish come up to a Royal Wulff drifting beneath a spruce tree rooted in granite left by ancient glaciers is to bathe my angler's soul in perfection.

Eastern Brook Trout

I have a passion for brook trout, particularly big brook trout. Near as I can tell my addiction began in childhood summers spent in Jasper park with my family. In those days the biggest of the brook trout were probably in Maligne Lake. Though there has been a paved road into Maligne for many years now, on my first trip there with my father in about 1965, you could only drive as far as the north end of Medicine Lake. From there you had to take a tour operator's boat across Medicine Lake and then take a four wheel drive minibus nine miles to the camp at Maligne Lake. We rented boats and motors at the camp and fished the lake in the rain for three or four days. Dad and I roared all over the lake but spent part of each day with the boat resting against the log boom that stretched across the river where it left the lake. We let the river current take our Williams Wabblers and worms down the river and into the mouths of the brook trout. The lake was producing plenty of two- to four-pound brookies in those days, and we caught our share. We had some extra excitement one day when the wind pushed the boat over the log boom and we headed down the river, but for once the outboard started first pull and we didn't have a wreck.

Brook trout are native to eastern North America, from the Hudson Bay area to Newfoundland and Labrador, and through the Appalachian mountains as far south as Georgia and South Carolina. They were first pursued for sport by eighteenth-century American anglers using wet flies and horsehair lines, and following in the tradition established in England by Izaak Walton and Charles Cotton. These pioneers must have been startled by the delicate beauty of these new fish that daintily plucked their flies from the hemlock shadows of Catskill and Adirondack streams to begin a new era in the history of fly-fishing.

Brook trout were introduced to Alberta when they were stocked in Banff National Park about 1910 and in Jasper's Maligne Lake in 1928. Today rainbow trout have largely taken over from brookies as the dominant fish in Maligne Lake, but there is still great fishing for big eastern brook trout in the Rockies, particularly in Fortress Lake just across the border from Jasper Park in British Columbia.

In Alberta's streams though, brook trout hold a much lower profile. They are, it seems, always the bridesmaids, never the bride. Brook trout rarely get big in our streams, but they often share the pools with other trout that do. Consequently the brook trout are usually remembered as a kind of after-thought: "Oh yeah, we caught a couple of little brookies too." West Stony Creek in the Red Deer system and upper Cataract Creek in Kananaskis Country are two streams where brook trout are dominant, but they are also common in Alford Creek and the upper portions of the North Raven River near the town of Caroline.

Some of the best places for brook trout are the beaver ponds of the western foothills—tangled still-water ponds with mucky bottoms and mazes of crisscrossed deadfall that make wading hard and casting harder. Some ponds maintain a population of wild fish while others are stocked regularly. It takes a particular personality to become a beaver pond specialist. You must be adept at reading and interpreting maps and proficient in the time-honored art of eavesdropping on other anglers. It also helps if you have a 4x4 with a large gas tank and don't object to some wild goose chases. For beaver ponds are not permanent fixtures. The beavers build them, they develop into fishy places and they eventually disappear, sometimes suddenly with floods like those in 1995, sometimes gradually with natural silting and deterioration. So a pond that's great today might not even exist tomorrow. Personal knowledge is the only absolute in this strange sport, and the maps and fishing guidebooks will rarely have the last word on the location of all the hot beaver ponds. For now though, there are numerous good ones in the upper Highwood River system and in the Tay and Raven systems in west central Alberta.

Brook trout belong to another time and place, and are often overlooked today by high-tech anglers who've been taught to seek bigger, stronger, more accessible fish. But an angler who is not stricken by the profound beauty of a wild brook trout is missing an important connection to the heart of our sport.

Mountain Whitefish

It's not quite true to say whitefish are a species with no tradition. It's just that the tradition has more to do with food gathering than sport. Throughout Alberta hordes of whitefish run up the creeks to spawn in the fall, and people follow close behind, catching them with a wide assortment of conventional and unconventional tackle in order to fill the smoker.

Mountain whitefish are probably the most abundant game fish in Alberta's streams. They are native to every river system and are found from the headwaters to the prairies. They are relatively easy to catch on flies and they grow big. Still, you'll find no eloquent descriptions of whitefish in angling literature nor elegant watercolors by famous artists. They're the Miss Congeniality of the fish world, and few fly-fishers consider them worthy of serious pursuit.

It is true that these "bonefish of the North" are a little hard to categorize. They don't have the noble fighting ability of a trout or the fierce disposition of a pike or muskie; neither are they viewed with the same repugnance as trash fish. Their appearance, too, is in-between: not as pretty as trout, not as ugly as suckers. A whitefish is always something of a disappointment to an angler who thinks he's hooked a trout. Even if it's a big one, nobody shouts, "Oh boy, it's a whitefish!" In Montana they don't even get the benefit of the doubt, for the angling limit there is a nice, tidy one hundred whitefish per day.

Alberta grows some of the largest mountain whitefish anywhere. The Athabasca River regularly produces huge fish, and in 1989 a Calgarian caught one in the Elbow River that weighed five pounds, six ounces, which made it the Alberta record at the time. Interestingly enough, the angler who caught it was twelve years old and the fish was eighteen. In 1991 a larger whitefish was taken from Gap Lake near Canmore.

Mountain whitefish are very abundant in some of our streams, and at times they get in the way of the trout we're trying so hard to catch. Yet they seem to operate on a slightly different schedule than the trout, and on those days when the trout pull their disappearing act, the whitefish sometimes remain cooperative and become a pretty decent consolation prize.

Whitefish are primarily but not exclusively bottom feeders, which makes them especially susceptible to a properly fished nymph. I consider them a good training fish for new fly-fishers. The highest concentrations of whitefish I know of are in the Crowsnest River, and in the Highwood and Sheep rivers, where the whitefish from the Bow gather to spawn in the fall.

Because the trout in Alberta's streams are not stocked, it's essential that mature fish be left to spawn and maintain the population. For these reasons I encourage anglers to release most of the trout—especially the larger ones—that they catch in Alberta's streams. Whitefish are naturally more prolific than trout though, and I don't think anyone's conscience should be offended by the thought of taking a limit for the smoker every now and then.

ARCTIC GRAYLING

I saw my first arctic grayling when I was sixteen or seventeen years old. A high school friend invited me to fish with him in the Swan Hills Country, where his father had a small logging operation. Though I'm not sure, I believe the stream we fished was the Freeman River. And while time has undoubtedly cast a favorable light on my memories, I do recall catching an awful pile of grayling. They were mostly small, in the eight- to ten-inch range, with a couple of trophies that measured thirteen. We caught them on dry flies, and I clearly remember watching purple shadows weave their way purposefully up from deep pools to grab a novice fly-tier's raggedy Black Gnat.

The arctic grayling is a fish with some notable ancestry. In fly-fishing's infancy the European grayling—a close relative of the Arctic version—shared both streams and status with the brown trout, and is mentioned frequently in glowing terms in early fly-fishing literature.

Arctic grayling are found throughout the northern hemisphere in rivers draining into the Arctic Ocean, including those in Russia, Siberia and Finland. They are beautiful fish, deserving their own category separate from trout. It's hard to talk about grayling without mentioning the huge, colorful dorsal fin that makes them so easy to identify, but their tiger-striped pelvic fins are nearly as stunning. They are almost exclusively insect-eaters and consequently love dry flies, usually showing a preference for small, dark patterns like the Adams and Black Gnat. Grayling are considered easy to catch, and in many areas their numbers have suffered because of it.

In Alberta, grayling are native to the Athabasca and Peace River systems. As a kid I caught tiny ones near Edson, and in recent years I've caught bigger ones in the huge Peace River itself near the British Columbia–Alberta border. And while there is still some good fishing in the Athabasca system, Alberta's best grayling streams are tributaries to the Peace River, most notably the middle and upper reaches of the Little Smoky River, east of the town of Grande Cache.

There are no grayling anywhere near large urban centers, or maybe it's that there are no large urban centers anywhere near grayling. Either way it's not a bad arrangement. Grayling are a part of Alberta's fishing heritage, and though their inability to tolerate proximity to human settlement has caused their decline in some places, such uncompromising need for wilderness is a large part of their attraction and charm. For nothing defines wilderness more completely than a healthy population of arctic grayling living and spawning in a river with no footprints in the gravel.

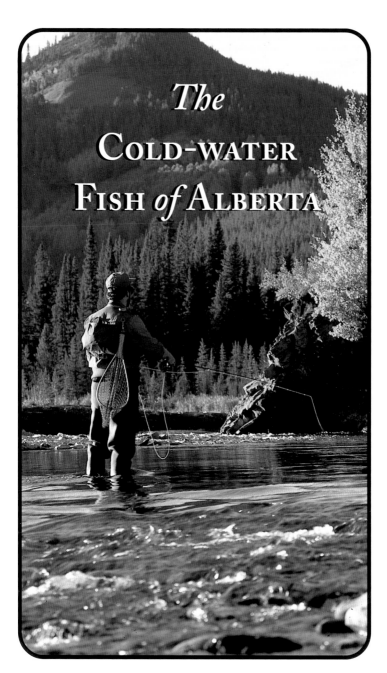

The
COLD-WATER
FISH *of* ALBERTA

Rainbow Trout

Rainbow trout can be identified by their black spots and the pink color on their gill covers and along their sides (though the pink is very pale in some cases). Their overall color varies from shiny silver to olive green. Rainbows are the strongest fighting trout, and anglers love the way they jump when hooked. Native only to the Athabasca system in Alberta, rainbows have been successfully introduced to every river system. Alberta's best rainbow streams are in the Bow and Oldman drainages.

Brown Trout

Brown trout have black, and sometimes red or orange, spots, but they lack the pink stripe of the rainbow. They are regarded as the most wary and difficult trout to catch. Browns are sometimes nocturnal, and the biggest ones are often caught after dark. The best brown trout fishing in Alberta is in the Bow River and in the foothill streams of the Red Deer and North Saskatchewan drainages.

Bull Trout

Bull trout are really members of the char family and are marked with light spots against an olive-green background. They can be distinguished from other char (eastern brook trout) by the absence of black markings on their dorsal fins. Bull trout are aggressive feeders and will often try to eat other fish nearly half their size. The bull trout fishing in southern Alberta is improving thanks to catch-and-release regulations, but some of the best bull trout fishing in the world is in the Peace River system of Northern Alberta.

Cutthroat Trout

Cutthroat trout are beautiful fish with heavy black spots and brightly colored gill covers. Their trademark is a slash of bright red or orange under the jaw. Equally beautiful are the wilderness streams where cutthroats live. Cutthroats are native to the Bow and Oldman river systems, but successful introductions have been made in the high country tributaries to the Red Deer and North Saskatchewan rivers.

Eastern Brook Trout

Many people consider the brook trout the most beautiful of the trout. Members of the char family, brook trout are distinguished by pale spots, green wormlike markings on their backs and white-edged fins. Brookies are native to eastern Canada but have been transplanted to numerous western lakes and beaver ponds. These delicate trout rarely grow large in our streams and as a result are often overlooked by anglers. They shouldn't be.

Mountain Whitefish

With their big scales and ventral mouth, whitefish are described as beautiful by few people. They do, however, have some redeeming characteristics: they are extremely abundant, relatively easy to catch (particularly on nymphs) and they grow big. Mountain whitefish are found in all Alberta drainages and are most abundant in faster, gravel–bottomed streams.

Arctic Grayling

No one can mistake arctic grayling for anything else, for their huge, colorful dorsal fins are unique. Their bodies are marked with subtle iridescent colors that seem to disappear when they are removed from the water. They are easy to catch and instill great confidence in new or young fly-fishers. Grayling are native to the Athabasca and Peace river systems in Alberta, and the best fishing is in Peace tributaries like the Wapiti and Little Smoky rivers.

3

The REQUIREMENTS
of STREAM TROUT

THE BASIC BUILDING BLOCKS of all life are water, oxygen, minerals and sunlight. Water may seem to be an obvious requirement, especially to a trout, but not just any water will do. It must be of the proper temperature, it must be free of toxic substances and it must carry oxygen and desirable minerals in quite specific volumes and proportions.

Oxygen must be present in the water at a concentration of at least four parts per million in order for trout to survive. However, water's ability to carry oxygen is dependent on its temperature, and the warmer the water the less oxygen it can carry. Ironically the warmer the water gets, the more oxygen trout need because they are cold-blooded creatures whose metabolic rate increases as the environment warms. In fact trout need about four times as much oxygen at 75° F as they do at 40° F, and this is very much a factor that determines where they can live. Trout need places where the dissolved oxygen level is consistently high or the water temperature is consistently cool or where there is some happy combination of both. Water temperature and oxygen content always go together, and when we read or hear about a fish kill caused by water that is too warm, it is often more accurately described as oxygen deprivation brought on by high temperature.

Plant life in the stream also affects the dissolved oxygen content of the water. Through photosynthesis, green plants produce oxygen in the daytime, which is beneficial to the trout. However, the same plants use oxygen at night, and too many of them in the stream can rob the water of oxygen during warm summer nights. It can be a case of too much of a good thing.

The food chain in a trout stream goes something like this: Trout eat aquatic insects, aquatic insects eat zooplankton, zooplankton eat green algae, and green algae "eat" minerals. Without the right minerals there are no algae, no chain and no trout. There are many beneficial minerals, but the most important are calcium and carbon. Calcium reacts with oxygen and carbon dioxide to produce calcium bicarbonate, which is the mineral most easily "eaten" by the green algae. Water high in calcium bicarbonate is alkaline and carries a healthy batch of green algae, large aquatic plants, aquatic insects and ultimately trout.

The final critical ingredient is sunlight, which is used by green plants to help convert inorganic chemicals into organic matter fundamental to the food chain. Most of Alberta's trout streams receive adequate sunlight, though occasionally suspended silt can inhibit sunlight's penetration and limit the growth of algae on the stream bottom.

With the essential building blocks in place we have a place where trout can survive. But the addition of some other ingredients can make the difference between surviving and thriving. The first of these is stability, the absence of sudden or severe fluctuations in either temperature or volume of flow. Stable temperature keeps the trout and its food free of dissolved oxygen deficiencies and promotes growth of a diverse insect community. Stable flow reduces the likelihood of flooding and the damage it can do to the stream bed and its plant and insect life.

Two other desirable ingredients in a trout stream are phosphorus and nitrogen. They act as fertilizers in the stream, just as they do on our lawns, stimulating plant production and promoting advanced growth throughout the food chain. Phosphorus and nitrogen can come from natural sources, like leaves and woody debris that fall into the water and decompose, or from artificial sources like cities and towns located along the waterway. Moderate amounts of these chemicals can be of great benefit to a trout stream, but excessive amounts can stimulate plant growth to the point where dissolved oxygen problems occur.

Other factors that enhance the productivity of a trout stream are an abundance of food and the presence of suitable habitat—neighborhoods where the fish have safety from predators and shelter from heavy current. Trout also need access to suitable spawning water either in their home stream or in a tributary to it.

The perfect trout stream would be cool, stable and somewhat alkaline, with lots of green plants growing both in and around the water. It would have abundant insect life as well as plenty of hiding places for trout and good spawning water nearby. That's a long checklist and not many streams make it on all counts. One type that does is a spring creek, so called because its source is an underground spring. The spring releases water of constant volume and temperature throughout the entire year. The water is high in calcium, and its alkalinity stimulates plant growth. In addition, a spring creek is not part of the drainage route for mountain snowmelt, and consequently it is unaffected by runoff. A spring creek's groundwater source keeps large portions of it free of ice in winter. Spring creeks, also sometimes called limestone or chalk streams, are among the most productive and celebrated trout waters in the world. Sadly Alberta has only a very small number of spring creeks, the most noteworthy being the North Raven River, northeast of Caroline.

Streams with more conventional snowmelt sources are called freestone streams, and most of Alberta's trout waters fall into this category. They are usually not as rich in minerals or as stable as spring creeks because of the nature of their sources. The best freestone streams, though, will have adequate mineral content and will undergo the inevitable seasonal changes in temperature and volume gradually rather than suddenly. This is often the case when the stream flows out of a lake or muskeg bog. The lake or swamp acts as a giant regulator, collecting snowmelt, adding minerals and releasing water to the outlet stream at a relatively constant rate. The Crowsnest River and some of the streams in the Peace River drainage are good examples.

Many people's image of trout fishing comes from the clichéd calendar photograph or beer commercial showing an angler knee-deep in the headwaters of an icy creek with majestic snow-capped mountains rising straight out of the water behind him. He is usually in the process of netting a six- or eight-pound rainbow. This looks wonderful, but I'm afraid it's mostly Madison Avenue stuff. If I were a complete skeptic I'd suggest that the photographer brought the huge trout with him as a prop.

Most streams like the ones in these photographs are not very productive and simply won't have many big fish in them. The reasons are many. The growing season in the headwaters is short, and the climate is harsh. The slope of such streams is often steep, the water velocity is high and runoff scours the stream bed each spring. Even in places where the slope is more gentle, the water probably freezes right to the bottom in winter. Most significantly though, the water here is nothing more than melted ice. It is very pure, carrying few minerals and little phosphorous or nitrogen. The only sources of nutrients in the headwaters are the plants growing along the stream. The result is that the typical high mountain stream has very little algae growth and a very weak food chain.

In Mother Nature's original plan, there was a fish capable of survival in these headwater areas. It is the bull trout, which has a voracious appetite and the ability to live long and grow large if man doesn't interfere. But as we have seen, man has been interfering with Alberta's bull trout for at least fifty years, and big ones are quite rare today in their original headwater range.

So while the headwaters are not the best of trout neighborhoods, neither are the extreme lower ends of Alberta's streams. A hundred miles from the mountains the rivers have slowed down and warmed up, and there are few riffles or rapids to inject oxygen into the water. They may now carry too many minerals because of the accumulated influence of cities, towns and irrigation. Perfect examples are the lower reaches of both the Bow and Oldman rivers in southeastern Alberta.

The middle sections of many of our streams, however, are a sweet compromise. As a stream moves from the mountains into the foothills, several significant things happen. Its slope, or gradient, declines, which increases the amount of suitable trout habitat. It enters a friendlier environment at a lower elevation, which provides a longer growing season and reduces the likelihood of freezing to the bottom. A foothill creek flows through forest or farmland, and its stream bed is composed of gravel, silt and soil instead of just rock as in its headwaters. Decaying leaves and plant material, animal waste and minerals wash in with the June rains, providing nutrients to stimulate green plant growth. The stream also may flow through geological formations, which leech calcium and other minerals into the water.

So trout fishers in search of Nirvana in Alberta will find it in the streams of the western foothills, near towns like Pincher Creek or Sundre or Grande Cache, where aspens and willows mingle with evergreens to provide shade, cover and nutrients to the trout. Knowledgeable fly-fishers are drawn to these gentle aromatic valleys, knowing that finding trout begins with finding trout habitat.

Fly-fishing is founded on the idea of trying to imitate the fish's natural food with an artificial fly, so it's helpful to know something about the creatures the fish eat. The next time you're on your favorite trout stream, turn over some rocks and see what the fish are eating. I do this when I teach a fly-fishing school, and everybody is always amazed that all those little wiggly things live under the rocks and in the weeds of the stream bed. Everybody crowds around to look, and somebody always says, "I had no idea there was so much stuff living in the creek." They're amazed but they shouldn't be. After all, the trout have to eat something or they wouldn't be there, and they have to eat other living things. Trout feed on anything and everything in the stream that is alive and smaller than they are.

Trout food falls into two basic categories: aquatic and terrestrial. Aquatic creatures are those that have to spend at least part of their life in the water. They can be aquatic insects, other fish or a miscellaneous group including leeches, freshwater crustaceans and aquatic worms. The most important of these are insects, and the most important trout stream insects are mayflies, caddisflies and stoneflies. Terrestrial creatures are those that are supposed to live entirely on land. The ones we're interested in (or more accurately the ones the fish are interested in) are those that live near the water but occasionally fall in. This group usually includes insects like grasshoppers, ants and beetles, but occasionally also includes things like clumsy mice.

Mayfly Adult

Mayfly Nymph

Aquatic insects are so called because they start their lives in the water. Mrs. Adult Bug lays her eggs on or in the water, and from the eggs come her immature children, called either nymphs or larvae, depending on which bug they are. The nymphs live in the water, feeding and growing until they are tired of being nymphs and are ready to become adults. This can take anywhere from a few months to a few years depending again on which bug.

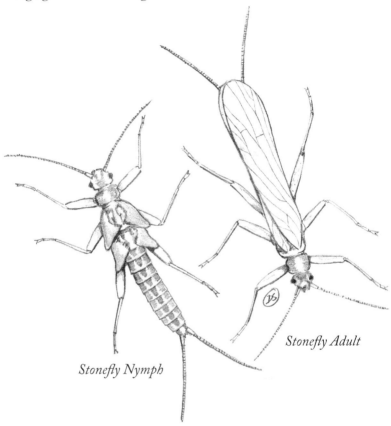

Stonefly Adult

Stonefly Nymph

At this point the three most important insects do things three different ways. Caddisflies seal themselves inside protective cases made of stream-bottom debris and undergo a transformation called pupation. The pupae then swim to the surface and shed their skin quickly to fly away as adults. In contrast, mayfly nymphs simply swim to the surface of the water where they split their skins and step out as adults, which are called duns. The duns float on the water, waiting for their wings to dry before flying away. A short time later the duns molt again to become sexually mature spinners, which have long tails and clear, sparkly wings. Stonefly nymphs can't swim, so they crawl to the edge of the stream and climb out on a rock or dead branch and make the change from nymph to adult on dry land. Once they've made it to adulthood the three bugs behave similarly again: They mate and the females lay eggs on the water and then die.

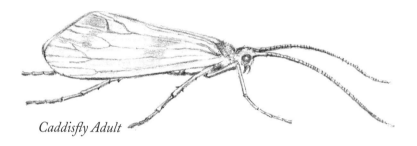

Caddisfly Adult

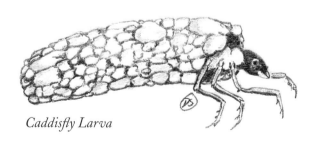

Caddisfly Larva

It's important to know that different bugs live in different types of water. For example, stoneflies only live in fast, rocky sections of freestone streams while some species of mayflies are only found in slow, silty areas. And within each group of insects there are different species that come in assorted sizes and colors.

As a verb, the word *hatch* is used to describe the moment of emergence of an aquatic insect. But it has also taken on a larger meaning as a noun to refer to the *event* of large numbers of a particular species of insect undergoing their emergence simultaneously, as in "the Green Drake hatch." On any stream the hatches will follow in the same order each year. So, just as the wolf-willows bloom in June but not in August, the *Tricorythodes* mayflies hatch in August but not in June. The correlation between the hatching of insects and the blooming of wildflowers can help you with your fishing, and the idea is outlined nicely in Bob Scammell's 1995 book, *The Phenological Fly: A Guide to Meeting and Matching the Super Hatches of the West.*

Every stream is a separate and distinct ecosystem with its own set of insects. So, while many streams share common insects, they may not have them in the same proportions. For instance, Prairie Creek and the North Raven River have both Green and Brown Drake mayflies. On the North Raven both bugs are abundant and important, but on Prairie Creek the Brown Drake is the main event and the Green is relatively minor. It's beneficial to know which bugs are important on which streams, and you can learn this from other anglers, books like this one or by studying the streams yourself.

The insects we imitate with our flies have become symbols of the sport, and a stylized mayfly on a hat, shirt pocket or somebody's letterhead is like a secret badge identifying the person as a fly-fishing sicko and linking him in spirit with other people similarly afflicted.

Fly-fishers have always studied the bugs that trout eat, and some people end up more interested in the bugs than the fish. That's fine, but it's not necessary to know the Latin name of the insect and the number of hairs on its kneecap in order to catch the fish that's eating it. If you know what the bug looks like, where it lives and how it moves, you can probably choose an imitation and fish it in a way that will fool the trout.

Above all, successful fly-fishing requires patient, careful observation of the interaction among water, fish and insects. To demonstrate, I want to show you the good stuff—how a little knowledge can be a dangerous thing . . . to the trout. Let's take an imaginary trip to a typical Alberta trout stream.

It's late June, we've just arrived and we need to decide what to do. We must take our clues from what we see, so we do our best to be observant. We look at the color and level of the water, we note the wind and the sky, and we check the air and the surface of the water for insect activity. But it's just a standard June morning, still a little cool, a few clouds, no breeze yet, no bugs on the water and, worst of all, no fish rising. Should we go home? I don't think so.

We walk until we come to a long section of fast water broken by big rocks. There are still no fish showing, but we notice that every big rock along the bank is speckled with leftover shucks from some kind of insect. These are stonefly nymph skins, and they could be just the clue we need. We know that for every empty shuck there is an adult stonefly around somewhere, and this tells us something about the fishing today and something else about the fishing a year from now. We know from the number of shucks on the rocks that a lot of adults are around, and we can presume that the fish will have seen and eaten some. They will have been conditioned to expect more today, so it makes sense to fish with an imitation of the adult stonefly.

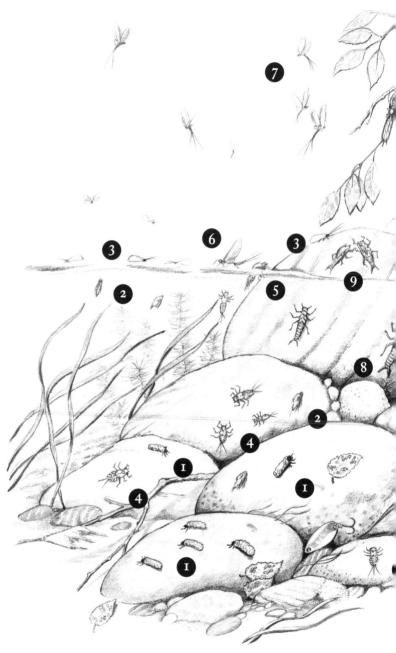

Insect Life Cycles in a Typical, Healthy Trout Stream

1   Caddis Larva

2   Emerging Caddis Pupae

3   Caddis Adult

4   Mayfly Nymphs

5   Emerging Mayfly

6   Mayfly Dun

7   Mayfly Spinners

8   Stonefly Nymph

9   Stonefly Shucks

10 Stonefly Adults

When we get home we make note of the date, water temperature and general weather conditions in our fishing diary because the same hatch will take place at about the same time next year. We might want to be on the stream just prior to the emergence next year because the fishing will probably be even better then. Why? Because of what we know about stoneflies. We know the nymphs live in fast water and must crawl to the edge of the stream and climb out on dry land before hatching into adults. So, in the week prior to the hatch, every mature stonefly nymph in the stream is heading for the edge. Many are knocked loose from the rocks by the fast water, and because they can't swim, they drift helplessly in the current. Guess who notices this? The trout see and eat more stonefly nymphs during the preemergence migration than at any other time of year, and the fishing with imitations of the nymph is usually spectacular.

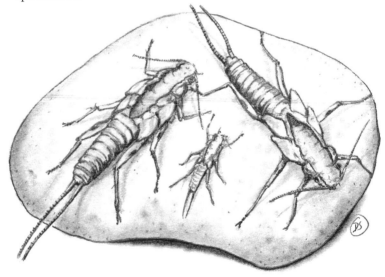

And that's how fly-fishing works. You develop a theory of what the fish are doing and try to confirm it by catching one on an imitation of their natural food. When you do catch a trout after this sort of sequential figuring, it is especially satisfying because you know *why* you caught him. Of course it's not always as straightforward as I've made it here, and there will be plenty of times when you feel more like Inspector Clouseau than Sherlock Holmes. But every once in a while all the pieces fall into place and you drift off to sleep that night knowing you're a genius.

4

The MECHANICS
of a TROUT STREAM

THE SKINLIKE BOUNDARY between air and water is what separates the trout's world from ours. The line is thin but absolute, and the fish's life is governed by many such immutable rules. Fish live in a medium heavy with pressure but devoid of gravity. Trout in streams must cope with the fact that their immediate environment is constantly moving. In order to understand trout, a fly-fisher must begin to understand the physical forces that define the trout's world.

Three laws of physics interact in moving water to create habitat for trout. Gravity tells the water to flow downhill, inertia tells it to flow in a straight line and friction, in turn, tells it to slow down where it touches the bottom and edges of the stream bed. In good streams this interaction helps create what I call character—places where the speed, depth, direction of flow and composition of the stream bottom and banks change frequently.

At a simple bend, for instance, the stream bed turns, but the water tries not to. It flows straight until it hits the bank and is forced to turn. Consequently the water is deeper and faster along the outside of the bend. The corner erases the monotony of straightness, replacing it with contrasts in speed, depth and direction. A meandering section of stream nearly always holds more fish than a long, straight section.

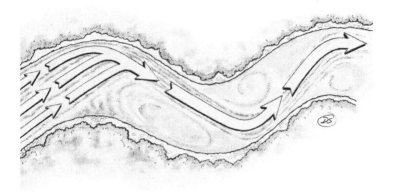

Water flows in a straight line until it is forced to turn. Water is deepest on the outsides of bends.

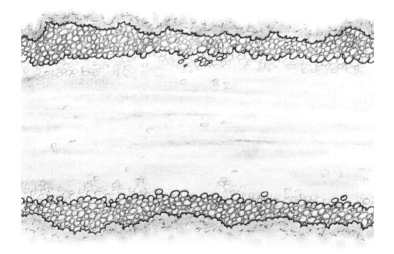

Featureless water has little character and few places for fish to live.

Trout in moving water always face into the current so water flows into their mouths and out their gills. This is the way things must be arranged in order for them to breathe. Fish also need two physical commodities from the stream: relief from strong current and safety from predators. Trout are strong swimmers, but they can't spend all their time on the constant treadmill of heavy current. They can feed in strong current, they can move through strong current, but they can't and won't stay in it without a reason.

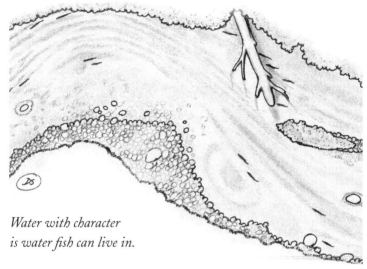

Water with character is water fish can live in.

Many people seem to know by intuition that fish need areas of quiet water to live in, but they often equate quiet water with big, slow pools. Fish don't need a huge expanse of quiet water—they need a slow spot bigger than they are, and that's all, providing their other needs are also met. There is always a narrow band of slower water along the bank and right next to the bottom of the stream because of friction between the water and the stream bed. Trout will often use these areas, especially if the stream bed is made of rock and cobble. An irregular bottom increases the effect of friction the same way coarse sandpaper does.

Other areas of lower velocity are places where something interrupts the flow of the current. The obvious sources of such relief are objects in the water like rocks, deadfall and weed beds, but they don't need to be huge. Even in rapids, a rock the size of a football will create a pocket of slow water large enough to hold a two-pound trout. Simple irregularities on the bottom or the bank can slow or deflect current as well. Remember how the ice gouged depressions in the gravel during spring breakup? These are also areas of lower velocity that trout will often use.

All this means that trout can and do live in the faster sections of streams, provided there are interruptions in the flow. Some people don't buy this though. I've often sent new fishers to water I know to be productive only to have them come back later and all but accuse me of sandbagging them. "That water's too fast," they say. "Fish can't live in that." Wrong. You must look not at the big picture of a river but at the multitude of closeup shots that tell you where the fish live.

Fish find relief from heavy current behind rocks and in depressions.

Fish also need safety from their predators, and their predators come from both within and above the water. Trout are most comfortable where they can't be easily seen. This can be in deep water or water with a broken surface. It can also be underneath something, like a fallen tree, undercut bank or weed bed. Many of the structures that provide safety from predators also provide relief from current, and when a fish has both he has a place to live, which anglers call a lie, (not to be confused with the other lie frequently associated with this sport), and the water is said to be holding water. Identifying lies is often referred to in fishing books as "reading the water."

Fish need to eat, and they eat differently in moving water than in still water. In lakes they feed the way people shop in a grocery store, cruising the aisles, looking for and picking up the stuff they like. In streams the water moves, so the fish don't have to. They choose places where food is concentrated and brought to them by the moving water, and simply pick up the good things that come by on the conveyor belt of current.

If the conveyor belt comes right by a fish's home—that is, if he has food, relief from current and safety all in the same place—he is in what we call a prime lie, which is the trout's equivalent of a ritzy condo downtown. The best of these are often undercut banks on the outsides of bends. A fish here truly has everything he needs. He's under the bank out of sight, he's tight against the edge where current is slowed by friction, and he's on the side of the stream where the current concentrates and delivers his food. Many of the smaller brown trout streams in the Sundre–Caroline region, like the North and South Raven rivers, are full of productive undercut banks.

Undercut banks are often prime lies.

On a large river, a prime lie might be a depression in the bottom a short distance below a riffle or along the seams where deep water meets shallow water or fast water meets slow water.

In most streams there are more fish than prime lies, so not every fish can have a perfect spot. Some fish will have safety and current relief at home, but will have to go out to eat. The restaurant is called feeding water. Fish will feed in places with less safety and current relief than they usually require if the food is abundant or easy to get, but they will move to the feeding water, eat and go home when they're done. These areas may change according to the type of food that's available; they could be along grassy banks in grasshopper season or in slow, shallow tailouts when mayflies or caddisflies are abundant. Feeding water is often hard to identify because it sometimes looks very ordinary. But if you see fish or evidence of fish in a place where they don't have both relief from current and safety, presume they're there to eat.

A number of years ago I fished a portion of the Crowsnest River with Vic Bergman, who spends more time on that stream than anyone I know. He took me to a piece of water I had fished many times previously by myself. We stopped at a slow tailout where the water flowed about eighteen inches deep over fine gravel. It was a cloudy September afternoon, and Vic said the Blue-winged Olives would begin to hatch and the fish would probably move in there to feed. They did, and they did. I caught a very good rainbow that was feeding nicely about three inches from the bank in eight inches of water.

When I asked Vic how he knew they would be there, he said that for years he had quickly bypassed this area by walking the path right along the bank, which is what I always did in this spot too. "Then one day I saw five or six wakes made by frightened fish leaving the bank as I walked by," he said. "The next time I stopped and waited below the tailout to see what was going on, and eventually I realized this was a place where the fish would come to feed." It's a perfect example of water used for feeding only, and of water that wouldn't be possible to identify until the trout helped us out.

This convoluted discourse is supposed to make it obvious where to fish in a stream, but in case I've missed the mark, let me lay out a plan.

1 First, look at the stream to see if any fish are feeding. If you see rises or flashes indicating fish feeding underwater, fish there. Always try for the fish you know are there before trying for the fish you think are there.

2 If there are no signs of feeding activity, try to identify the prime lies in the stream, and concentrate on them with a method that makes sense for the stream and the time of year.

3 Fish to the holding water. Even if a fish isn't in the habit of feeding from his holding lie, he probably will if you make it easy for him.

If none of the above works—and plenty of times it won't— you can always resort to the contemplative approach, and lie down with your hat over your eyes and have a nap.

If wild trout are to continue to thrive in a stream, they must spawn, and they're quite choosy about where and when they do it. Rainbows, cutthroats and arctic grayling spawn in the spring, while brook, brown and bull trout, as well as mountain whitefish, spawn in the fall.

The factors that trigger spawning are a combination of photoperiod (the amount of sunlight per day) and water temperature. Some species spawn near their summer water while others migrate—usually upstream—to where they find water of the right temperature, speed, depth and bottom composition. Trout often spawn in the tailouts of pools, where the gravel is free of silt and fairly loosely packed. The water in these areas can flow through the gravel rather than just over top of it, thereby providing the developing eggs with a good supply of oxygen as well as removing metabolic waste from the eggs.

Eggs spawned in the spring hatch soon after, and the fry feed and grow through the summer. Eggs laid in the fall spend the winter in the gravel of the stream bed and hatch the following spring. Both spring and fall spawners encounter some obstacles to success. The survival of eggs spawned in the spring is influenced by the timing and severity of spring runoff, and fall spawners' eggs can easily be destroyed by anchor ice in a cold winter.

Something rarely discussed in even the best trout fishing books is what trout do in winter. It's probably because very little is known about the topic, particularly in areas like Alberta, where the winters are usually long and harsh. Fish still need food, shelter and safety, but in winter the stream may not give it to them in the same ways or in the same places it does in the summer.

One of the most obvious things to affect fish behavior in winter is ice, which can form in a stream in a couple of different ways. When the air temperature drops through the fall and early winter, ice forms on the surface of the slowest water first, eventually creating a roof over the stream. This then insulates the water beneath from the effects of the cold air above. But if the air becomes extremely cold the water temperature can actually drop *below* 32° F. This is known as super-cooling and can cause the formation of frazil ice, which is formed of disk- or needle-shaped ice crystals that stick to one another and to debris in the stream and sometimes lodge in the gills of fish. A buildup of frazil ice leads to the formation of anchor ice, which adheres to the stream bottom and can build up until it blocks the flow of the water. Obviously fish must move to places in the stream where this doesn't happen.

In an innovative study done in 1991–92, Richard Brown and Slav Stanislawski of the University of Alberta observed the wintertime activities of cutthroat trout in the North Ram River and two of its tributaries west of the town of Rocky Mountain House. Fish were caught and implanted with radio transmitters so their movements could be monitored through the winter.

The scientists noted many interesting things. Fish living in pools with springs entering stayed there through the winter, for the springs keep the water temperature above the point of frazil- and anchor-ice formation. Fish living in pools subject to anchor-ice buildup were forced to move, some of them twice. About mid-September they began to shift from a feeding mode to an energy-conserving mode and moved from shallower summer lies to gather in deeper pools with a lot of cover in the form of deadfall and beaver caches. But by late October anchor ice had begun to form on the debris in those pools, and the fish were forced to move to areas where groundwater kept the temperature up or where thick ice covered the surface of deep water. Some fish bypassed the intermediate step and moved directly to the final wintering pools.

In a subsequent study on a small tributary to the Oldman River, Richard Brown noted some differences in fish behavior caused by the extreme variability in winter weather in this part of Alberta. The fish moved into wintering pools when anchor ice formed, but when Chinook weather warmed the water and melted the ice, the fish moved back out. This can happen several times through a typical winter in Chinook Country. So the winter environment may be more stressful here than in an area that gets cold in the fall and stays cold until spring.

The availability of adequate winter habitat is a factor which influences every stream's productivity. Some people feel that a lack of good wintering water is the reason some of the brown trout streams southwest of Red Deer are capable of producing big, healthy trout but not in high numbers. And it is probably no coincidence that two of our most productive streams, the Bow and Crowsnest rivers, both receive the warming influence of human occupation along their banks.

To paraphrase Kermit the Frog, it's not easy being long and slippery, particularly if you live in the harsh surroundings of an Alberta stream. Thankfully though, these critters called trout are a hardy, resilient lot and tough enough to survive the worst of what Mother Nature and anglers throw at them.

5

CHASING
ALBERTA TROUT

SOMEBODY ONCE SAID there are two types of fishing: fly-fishing and everything else. And though it might sound a little uppity, there is some truth to the statement, which will be apparent if we compare fly-fishing with other methods.

All non–fly-fishing outfits work on the same principle, and it goes something like this: A weight is tied to the end of a thin, light line, and a rod is used as a flexible lever to throw the weight out into the water. As the weight travels through the air it pulls line off the reel.

This arrangement works fine until you replace the weight with a tiny, fluffy trout fly and try to cast it. A spinning outfit won't cast a fly because there is almost no weight in the object being thrown (after all, you can't throw a feather). But with a fly-casting outfit the thick fly line itself provides the weight needed to make a cast, and the tiny, fluffy trout fly simply goes along for the ride because it's attached to the line. This is the fundamental difference between a fly-fishing outfit and all other types of tackle. Put simply, a spinning rod casts the weight at the end of the line, and a fly rod casts the line itself.

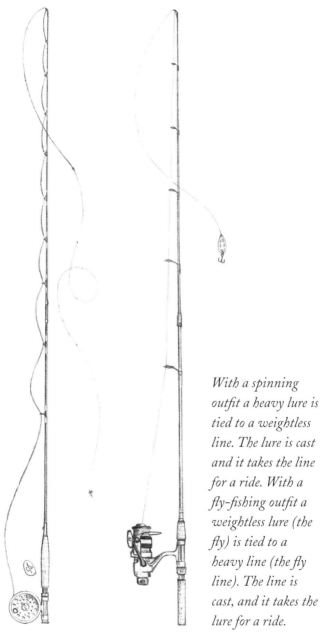

With a spinning outfit a heavy lure is tied to a weightless line. The lure is cast and it takes the line for a ride. With a fly-fishing outfit a weightless lure (the fly) is tied to a heavy line (the fly line). The line is cast, and it takes the lure for a ride.

There is a significant philosophical difference between fly-fishing and other methods too. When we use a spoon or spinner we're putting a small, cleverly designed machine into the water. This machine interacts with the pressure of the water to move in an erratic way that attracts the fish's attention and incites the strike response. Most of the work is done by the lure. When we use bait we're showing the fish an actual food item—something that looks, feels, smells and tastes real because it is. When the fish eats the bait it discovers our devious surprise hidden inside. Most of the work is done by the worm.

Fly-fishing is different. Because we are imitating the trout's natural food with our artificial fly, we are in essence agreeing to play by the fish's rules. We first make a speculation about what the fish is eating and then show it an artificial fly in a way that will convince it that the fly is just another mayfly or grasshopper like those it has been eating all afternoon. Fly-fishing thus rewards knowledge and understanding, and this is why it's so satisfying to catch fish on a fly—most of the work is done by the angler. Fly-fishing is not better than bait- or spin-fishing, but it's more more fun, and that is all the reason we really need.

Nothing about fly-fishing is difficult, but nearly everything about it is different, and in order to do it one must know a little about the tools of the trade.

TACKLE

Lines

Fly lines are thicker and heavier than monofilament spinning lines, and some fly lines are thicker and heavier than others. The weight of the fly line is identified with a number between 1 and 15. There is a line built to correspond to each number, and as the numbers get higher the lines get heavier. Note that a number 6 fly line (also called 6-weight) is not a 6-pound line. The number designates weight, *not* breaking strength.

If you're selecting fly tackle, the first decision to make is the weight of the fly line, and that's determined by the type of fishing you're going to do. A light fly line, in the 1- to 4-weight range, is beneficial in small, clear streams, where finesse is important. A heavy fly line, like an 8- or 9-weight, is best where power is essential. This might be when fishing big flies on a big lake in a big wind. If the word *big* crops up more than a couple of times in the description of the fishing you're going to do (other than the inevitable reference to the size of the fish you plan to catch) you might need a heavy line.

The first fly line to buy is a floating line. It is more versatile than a sinking line because it can be used with both floating (dry) and sinking (wet) flies. If you fish small streams exclusively, you'll probably never need anything but a floating line. If you fish big rivers or lakes though, you might someday find a sinking or sink-tip fly line helpful for certain types of wet-fly fishing.

The fly line should be tapered in either weight-forward or double-taper configuration. Lines with no taper are called level lines, and though they are inexpensive they should be avoided because they simply won't cast properly.

Rods

The second component to select is the fly rod. It's essential to understand that each fly rod is designed to cast a particular weight of fly line, so be sure to get a rod made to cast the line weight you've chosen. This is *very* important. If you mismatch the rod and line, the outfit might behave so poorly that you might give up on the whole idea of fly-fishing.

Today there is no reason to consider a rod made of any material but graphite. Adequate graphite fly rods are now available at a wide range of prices. Get the best one you can afford from a dealer who can help you make a good choice.

It's not hard to imagine an Alberta fly-fisher casting dry flies on a small brown trout stream in the morning and trying to dredge up rainbows from a deep, cold lake the same afternoon. And while many of us eventually end up with different tackle for different types of fishing, most prefer to start with a single outfit that is versatile and capable of handling a variety of situations. The fly-fisher who wants one outfit to fish Alberta's streams comfortably and effectively should choose a rod between eight and nine feet long that casts a 5- or 6-weight line. Such an outfit is powerful enough to handle the majority of the big-river fishing yet delicate enough to be efficient on the smaller creeks.

Reels

A single-action reel with an adjustable drag is what ninety-eight percent of Alberta's fly-fishers use. *Single action* means there is a direct connection between the reel handle and the reel spool—no slipping clutches or multiplying mechanisms. The handle turns in one direction to retrieve line onto the reel and in the opposite direction when line is pulled off the reel.

All modern fly reels have removable spools. Be sure you can buy spare spools separately in case you decide to get a second line later. This is a subtle plug for name-brand reels that have been on the market for some time. If a reel has proved successful, both performance-wise and sales-wise, it will probably continue to be available in the future. The same is not always true for the "new and improved" techno-reels.

Fly reels come in different sizes, and you should get one that will hold the fly line you've already chosen, plus between fifty and one hundred yards of braided Dacron backing, which goes on the reel before the line. The fly line is about thirty yards long, which is more than enough for casting but occasionally less than enough for fighting a fish. Backing gives you the additional length you sometimes need to play a hard-running fish. Don't leave home without backing on your reel. You don't need it often, but when you need it you need it bad.

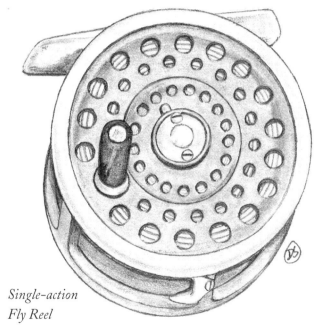

Single-action Fly Reel

The fly reel is not involved in casting or retrieving, and its job is simply to store the line and release it smoothly without overrunning itself. Of course it should be reliable, but if you're on a restricted budget it makes sense to put the majority of the dollars into the rod and the line because they do the majority of the work.

Leaders

The most confusing part of the fly-fishing outfit is the leader. It is the semi-invisible link between the fly line and the fly. The fly line is too thick and too visible to be attached directly to the fly, so we use a piece of nylon monofilament between them. Like the fly line, the leader must be tapered—thick at the end that attaches to the line, thin at the end that attaches to the fly. The fat end of the leader is called the butt and the skinny end the tippet.

There are three common types of tapered leaders. One is called a knotted or compound leader, which is a series of pieces of monofilament tied together, each piece thinner than the previous one. A knotless leader is just that—one piece of monofilament that is thick at one end and thin at the other. A braided butt leader has a tapered butt section made of fine, braided monofilament fibers and a single piece of monofilament for the tippet. The most popular leader lengths are seven and one-half, nine and twelve feet.

Three Leaders: (clockwise from left) compound, knotless, braided butt.

There is a critical relationship between the diameter of the leader tippet and the size of the fly tied to it. The tippet must be fine enough to allow the fly to move naturally in the water but not so fine that the strength of the knot is jeopardized. So it's hard to choose a leader until you know what fly you're going to fish with. Most fly-fishers carry a few leaders of different lengths and tippet diameters, and also spools of tippet material so they can replace just the tippet rather than the whole leader when a major change in fly size is needed.

MATCHING TIPPET DIAMETER TO FLY SIZE

Tippet Diameter	Fly Sizes
0X (.011 inches)	2, 4
1X (.010 inches)	4, 6
2X (.009 inches)	6, 8
3X (.008 inches)	8, 10
4X (.007 inches)	12, 14
5X (.006 inches)	16, 18
6X (.005 inches)	20, 22
7X (.004 inches)	22, 24

The rod, reel, line, leader and fly are the major components of the fly-fishing outfit, but there are other things nearly as essential. They include fly floatant, leader snippers, forceps and a hook sharpener. Most of us carry these along with our flies, leaders and tippet material in a fishing vest or chest pack, which keeps everything handy yet leaves our hands free to cast and haul in huge numbers of huge fish. Unless you have a high tolerance to cold water you'll also probably want to wear waders when you fish in streams.

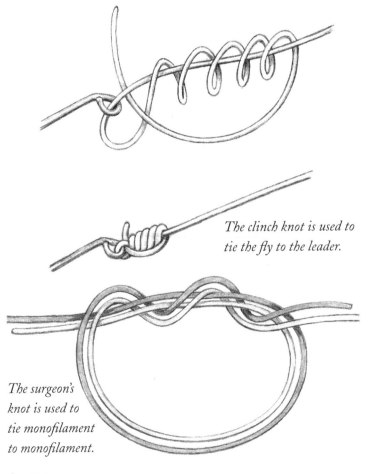

The clinch knot is used to tie the fly to the leader.

The surgeon's knot is used to tie monofilament to monofilament.

BOATS

Fly-fishers are big on theories, especially the one that involves greener grass: "If I could cast just a little farther or wade a just a little deeper or get to that little island in the middle of the river somehow, I *know* I'd catch more fish." This, I'm told, is an ancient human trait, and if that's true I'll bet it started with the invention of the world's first boat. It was probably the head fisherman in the cave who bore the brunt of everybody's jokes as he put the finishing touches on his new creation that was going to allow him to catch more and bigger fish than anybody else in the tribe. And ever since, fishers and boats have gone together like gasoline and matches. Okay, bad example.

Fly-fishers sometimes use boats in moving water, both as casting platforms and as transportation to less accessible water. While almost any boat will work in almost any lake, it's not quite that simple in moving water. Some streams are simply too small for a boat, and some water is downright dangerous if the wrong kind of boat is used.

A McKenzie River Driftboat, popular on the Bow River.

Flat-bottomed aluminum Johnboats and dory-shaped McKenzie River Driftboats made of aluminum, fiberglass or wood are the most popular boats for floating Alberta's rivers. Some inflatables are also suitable. If you want to see these types of craft in action, visit the Bow River below Calgary. They are also occasionally used on other portions of Alberta rivers like the upper Bow, the Red Deer below the Dickson Dam, the Clearwater, and the Oldman below the Oldman Dam. These boats are usually controlled by oars alone though motors can be used in certain circumstances. Canoes can also be used comfortably in many Alberta rivers. They are quick and maneuverable but somewhat difficult to fish from.

If you want to put a boat or canoe into a river there are some important things to consider before doing it for the first time. Steering and controlling a watercraft is a different game in moving water, and it's best to get help from an experienced friend before you make your first solo trip. Be certain that the boat and its captain are capable of handling the particular piece of water you've chosen. Know how far it is to your take-out point downstream, and know what the take-out point looks like. Be sure to arrive there before dark. Ask in advance about the location of obstacles or difficult water.

You'll either need to have someone pick you up at the end of your trip or have a vehicle waiting at the take-out point when you get there. You can move the vehicle yourself prior to your trip if you enlist the help of a friend with a second vehicle. On the Bow River below Calgary there are people who provide vehicle shuttles for a small fee. You can contact them through fly shops in Calgary.

Recently another type of water craft has developed, and I don't know if it even has a generic name yet. Sometimes called a pontoon boat or a kick boat, it's a variation on the lake fisher's float tube. Unlike the float tube though, it is intended for use in moving as well as still water. A kick boat has two inflatable pontoons with a rigid frame separating them and keeping them parallel. The fisher sits on the frame and kicks his feet (with fins on) to steer and move the craft. It can be equipped with many options, including oars and even an outboard motor.

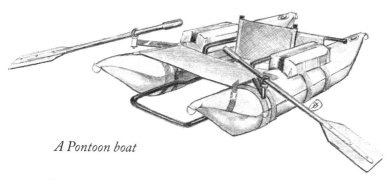

A Pontoon boat

Though people sometimes use float tubes in rivers, it's not a practice I recommend in any but the slowest and gentlest of streams. I don't recommend them in the Bow River.

LEARNING TO FLY-FISH

While it is theoretically possible to learn to fish by trial and error, it is much easier to learn from another person who already knows how. The problem is that the other person is probably a husband, father, uncle or friend who, while agreeing to teach you, is really more interested in fishing than in showing you how.

There are other choices. Courses and fly-fishing schools are often offered through tackle shops, fishing clubs, colleges, and parks and recreation departments of Alberta's cities. Organizations like the Federation of Fly Fishers and Trout Unlimited occasionally sponsor seminars or workshops with well-known fly-fishing instructors and celebrities (yes, there are fly-fishing celebrities).

If a fishing school isn't for you, there are dozens of instructional books available. Today's books are better than those of fifteen or twenty years ago, and two of the best are *The Orvis Fly Fishing Guide* by Tom Rosenbauer and *Fly Fishing Basics* by Dave Hughes. Video is proving to be a very successful medium of instruction for everything from rifle shooting to gourmet cooking. Two good, basic fly-fishing videos are *Fly Fishing for Trout* with Gary Borger and *Learning to Fly Fish* with Jack Dennis.

The one area in which video is far superior to a book is in the teaching of casting. Learning to fly-cast from a book is like taking dance lessons over the phone. My favorite instructional fly-casting video is *Basic Fly Casting* with Doug Swisher.

Reconnaissance

The best asset a fly-fisher can have is specific, local, up-to-date information on the water he is about to fish. One way to get this information is to buy it by hiring a guide. This is the quickest path to success on unfamiliar water. The other way is to collect the information yourself by making a commitment to a new area and spending plenty of time learning about it on your own. It takes much longer this way, but many people consider it part of the challenge and indeed part of the satisfaction of fly-fishing.

If you don't want to hire a guide (or if none are available in the area you're interested in) and you don't have time to figure things out completely on your own, you'll need to get some information from other sources. There is an art to investigating a new fishing spot, and some people are just naturally good at it. A friend of mine has found some of his best spots by hanging around tackle shops and eavesdropping on other anglers while pretending to browse through the magazines. If you prefer a more straightforward approach, ask at your local tackle shop, sporting goods store or library for books, pamphlets, magazines and videos containing information on the area you're interested in.

While tackle shops and fishing clubs are likely the best sources of up-to-date local knowledge, you'll need to understand the protocol involved in obtaining information. Many people are protective and secretive about their favorite places to fish. It's called the Frenchman's Creek philosophy, whereby all good streams are called that in order to hide their true identity. While you may or may not agree with this, you're going to run into it, and you'll have to respect it if you want to get anywhere.

What this means is that you'll encounter some serious resistance if you swagger into the next meeting of the Slippery Trout Chasers Club and immediately announce to the group that you're new to the area and would appreciate it if each member could draw a couple of detailed maps to terrific fishing spots and pass them on to you at the end of the meeting.

Instead you need to go slowly. Get to know the people with the information, and establish credibility with them. Probably the best way to do this is to make a point of not asking them where they fish. The old-timers especially will notice this, and it will be a mark in your favor. You'll find most experienced fly-fishers helpful and willing to get you off on the right track if you don't push them too far.

Other people who can help are Fish and Wildlife officers and provincial or national park wardens. Ask your fishing friends what they know about your chosen area and who they'd go to for information about the place.

It's important to do as much of this homework as possible in advance of your first visit to a new place. It's also a good idea to get some maps of the area, which are almost as essential as good tackle. Excellent provincial government maps are available from numerous map stores in Edmonton and Calgary, but I've come to rely on a series of eight maps, collectively called *The Fishin' Map*, which are available at tackle shops throughout the province. They show roads, trails, cutlines, campgrounds and species of fish in each body of water. All major cold-water drainages except the Peace are covered in this series.

When to Fish

Should I give you the smart-aleck answer? I will because it also happens to be the best answer: Fish whenever you can. The worst fishing you'll ever have will be better than a lot of other things you'll do in this life, so never pass up a chance to go fishing. Having said that, let me add that you'll probably catch more fish if you do it at certain times and under certain circumstances.

You should fish when the fish are feeding. That sounds simple, but when do they feed? They feed when their food is especially abundant or easily obtained. This might be during a major hatch of aquatic insects or on a warm, windy August afternoon when a lot of grasshoppers are being blown onto the water. Fish also eat when they're hungry, which they'll be after something has prevented them from feeding for a while. This might be when they first return from spawning or when the water finally warms up after a long cold winter.

Rainbow and brown trout are somewhat sensitive to bright sun, and fishing for them is usually best on cloudy days or before or after the sun is directly on the water. Conversely, cutthroat trout usually live in colder water, and seem to prefer to feed on warm sunny days when water temperature is at its highest.

There's one more item to factor into the equation. Doug Swisher and Carl Richards call it the "pleasant time of day" theory. There is a water temperature range at which fish are most active, and the water often reaches that point at the time of day when people are most comfortable outdoors. On cold days early and late in the season, the fish will be active only when the water temperature finally climbs up into their preferred range. This will be in the afternoon, when the anglers will also be most comfortable. Conversely, during a hot summer, the water temperature may rise above the trout's ideal range in the middle of the day, so the fish will be active early in the morning, before the water becomes too warm, and later in the day, when it cools off, which again are the times when people are most comfortable. This theory holds up especially well on smaller bodies of water that undergo fairly large daily temperature changes. The effect is less dramatic on big rivers. All this having been said, it is usually nearly hopeless to try to fly-fish when streams are extremely dirty from runoff or heavy rain.

Trout Stream Etiquette

There are a lot of people taking up fly-fishing these days, and many people learn the skills of the sport quickly because so much information is readily available. The one area, though, in which the instructional media fails is in the teaching of etiquette. Though I hate the analogy, a trout stream is like a golf course—at least in that a code of behavior among participants is better than total anarchy.

In some parts of the East, a trip to the trout stream is like stopping at the country club after work: You can get some fresh air, chat with fellow members about something other than business and relax with a drink when everybody's done. The solitude part of the fly-fishing experience has long since disappeared in these places. In the West, especially in Alberta, it has not, and in fact solitude is fiercely and jealously guarded as one of the things that separates our fishing from theirs. Behavior that would be accepted and indeed expected on the Beaverkill River in New York might get a hostile response in Alberta.

Trout stream etiquette usually boils down to the amount of space that should be left between different parties of anglers. This is built on a sliding set of criteria. Protocol is different in different places, depending on the number of fishers using the streams. On eastern streams in Pennsylvania or New York state or even on heavily fished western rivers like the Frying Pan in Colorado, it is acceptable to share a pool with someone who is not a member of your party, but try it in Alberta or most other parts of the West and you'll find you've ruined someone's day.

Problems begin when someone encroaches on another person's space. The question then is how much space does a person need, or perhaps more realistically, how much space is a person entitled to expect?

While nobody has appointed me to be in charge of such things, this is my book, so here are my thoughts on this question and others regarding etiquette for Alberta trout streams:

1 Give the other fly-fisher as much room as you'd like to have yourself. The golden rule works.
2 On smaller streams it's imperative to stay out of the pool another angler is fishing or resting and a good idea to stay out of his sight altogether.
3 On a big river stay well out of speaking voice range of other fishers.

4 Stay away from the bank of the stream when you know another angler will be fishing that water soon.

5 If you are working your way up or down a stream and you encounter a stationary angler or an angler working his way toward you, stop fishing before you enter his space, get out of the water and circle well beyond him before continuing to fish.

6 If you need to cross private land to get to the water, obtain permission from the landowner. If you can get to the stream without crossing private land (usually from a bridge) you can legally fish and move up or downstream if you stay between the high-water marks on the banks. While you are not legally bound to gain permission as long as you follow this procedure, courtesy demands that you talk to a landowner if you plan to start your fishing near his home.

7 If someone takes you to a favorite fishing spot in confidence, respect that confidence. Don't take someone else there without consulting the other angler first.

In many places throughout the West, there are conflicts between wading and boating fishers. The only place in Alberta where there is potential for this to happen with any regularity is on the Bow River downstream of Calgary. The problem arises because both wading and boating fishers like to concentrate on the water near the banks—the waders from the bank side out and the boaters from the river side in. In this situation the pedestrian anglers have the right of way, and boats should move well away from the bank in the area near the wading fishers. Boaters should bypass as much water as the wading angler can comfortably fish in half an hour before moving the boat back near the bank.

One problem occurs on the Bow when anglers take their

drift boats down small side channels in the river. From the top of a channel it's often impossible to see if there are other fishers wading in it farther down. When a boat suddenly encounters a wading fisher in a tight channel, the boater then has no choice but to float right through the water the fisher is working. The floater gets embarrassed and the wader gets irate. The solution is to keep boats out of the smaller side channels. Stop and fish them on foot.

Powerboaters should move to the far side of the river when going upstream past a wading angler. When going downstream they should kill the motor and drift past.

It's easy to get caught up in the tools and trappings of fly-fishing and to suddenly find that you're a competitor in the "he who collects the most toys wins" game. When I went to New Zealand to fish for the first time in 1989 I immediately noticed a contrasting attitude toward our sport. While we North Americans demonstrated our unwavering obsession with the technicalities of tackle and technique, the Kiwi guides made it clear that their love affair is still with the rivers and the trout. It's something I try to remember.

Part 2

Streams, Flies & Dreams

*T*HE NEXT FIVE CHAPTERS *are personal examinations of each major Alberta river system. My objective here is not to direct anglers to specific pools on specific streams, but rather to provide information that will be useful throughout each drainage. There are a number of good publications available that provide information on every stream. One of the best is* The Alberta Fishing Guide, *an annual magazine published by Barry Mitchell Publications in Red Deer. Widely available beginning about mid–March of each year, it contains maps, listings of thousands of lakes and streams throughout the province and articles on all types of fishing in Alberta.*

To a fly-fisher the two most important roads in Alberta are secondary Highway 22 between the Crowsnest Pass and Rocky Mountain House, and the Forestry Trunk Road that extends from Coleman to Grande Prairie. The trunk road carries different designations in different areas and is variously identified as Highway 40 and 940 in southern Alberta and Highway 734 in the Peace Country. Portions of it also are simply identified as the Forestry Trunk Road. It is an all-weather, mostly gravel road that varies somewhat in quality.

The angling regulations in many parts of Alberta are rather complex. In many ways this is good, for it's a sign that different fisheries are being examined individually. Some Alberta streams are under complete no-kill regulations. Other streams are under no-kill part of the time, and some others yet are under standard provincial regulations that allow the killing of five fish per day. All this puts a significant onus on the angler to be sure of the regulations before fishing. Please don't rely on the general summaries occasionally presented in this book, for the rules constantly evolve in response to changing conditions. Always check before you fish.

While killing fish for food is not immoral, there are few moving water fisheries in Alberta that will not benefit from a volun-

tary catch-and-release philosophy, particularly on trout and grayling. You don't need to worry about complex creel limits if you simply put them all back.

Fly-fishers in the eastern United States have been studying trout stream insects for many decades, and even inexperienced anglers can easily find out about the sequence and importance of the insect hatches on their favorite streams. Alberta, however, is still a frontier in the fly-fishing world, and with a few exceptions like the Crowsnest River's salmonfly hatch, little of our insect information has yet reached the realm of common public knowledge. Much of it is still being gathered and catalogued by anglers. Consequently we are in some ways pioneers, exploring only partially charted territory, still hoping to discover new, important hatches. A recent example of this is Bob Scammell's confirmation in 1993 of the presence of North America's largest mayfly—Hexagenia limbata *(no, not the dance)*— in a couple of streams in the Rocky Mountain House region, something he reported on in his latest book, The Phenological Fly.

And there are undoubtedly other important hatches yet to be discovered in Alberta. So the hatch charts that accompany each of the next five chapters, then, are not complete. They simply represent one point in the evolution of understanding that is still in progress. The dates shown on the charts are approximate, and actual dates will vary with elevation and weather. I can hear nervous fly-fishers all over the province breathing a collective sigh of relief: "Good, McLennan doesn't know about the great Ephemerella prontosaurus hatch on Frenchman's Creek yet."

6

The OLDMAN RIVER SYSTEM

THE SOUTHWESTERN CORNER of Alberta seems like a small earthly sample of heaven to many of us fly-fishers today, but we are hardly the first to feel that way. For the last century ranching families have given thanks for the bounty provided by endless grasslands waving under warm Chinook winds. And for centuries before that the Blackfoot and Peigan Indians knew the headwaters of the Oldman River to be the home of Na'pi, the Great Spirit and provider.

The trout waters in the Oldman River drainage are among Alberta's best. Virtually all flowing waters in the foothill portion of the drainage carry trout and whitefish and provide good to superb fishing.

THE BIG PICTURE

The streams in the Oldman system are generally small- to medium-sized with the exception of the lower Oldman itself, which is a good-sized river. Most are very clear with boulder and gravel stream beds, deep pools and fast pocket water. The gradients are often fairly steep, particularly in the upper reaches.

The upper Oldman and its major northern tributary, the Livingstone River, begin near the Continental Divide southwest of Calgary. Both are very good cutthroat and bull trout streams, and the Livingstone should get even better with the recent introduction of no-kill regulations. The two rivers flow south before joining and flowing eastward through a narrow slot in the Rockies aptly called the Gap. Downstream of the Gap rainbow trout begin to appear as the river winds eastward through a beautiful piece of ranch country called the Whaleback. The river bends south again, and by the time it approaches and enters the Oldman Reservoir, rainbows have become the dominant fish. The Crowsnest River enters the same reservoir from the south, as does the Castle River a little farther to the east.

The Castle is a fine stream for cutthroats and rainbows, and is made up of a number of equally appealing tributaries, including Lynx Creek and the Carbondale River, both of which are good cutthroat and bull trout streams. The West Castle is noted for its willing cutthroats and the fact that it stays clear when most other streams in the area are muddy from heavy rain. Stretches of the West and South Castle were formerly accessible from rough logging roads, but the spring floods of 1995 took portions of these roads out, and it is unlikely they will be rebuilt, at least not in the near future. This will probably make the fishing even better for those who don't mind hiking in.

Downstream of the reservoir the Oldman River dodges to avoid the south end of the Porcupine Hills and moves out across flatter ground through the Peigan Indian Reserve, past Head-Smashed-In Buffalo Jump and through the town of Fort Macleod.

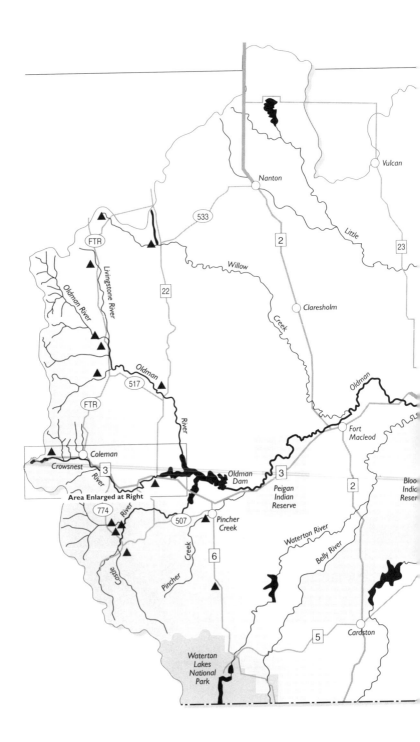

Oldman River Basin

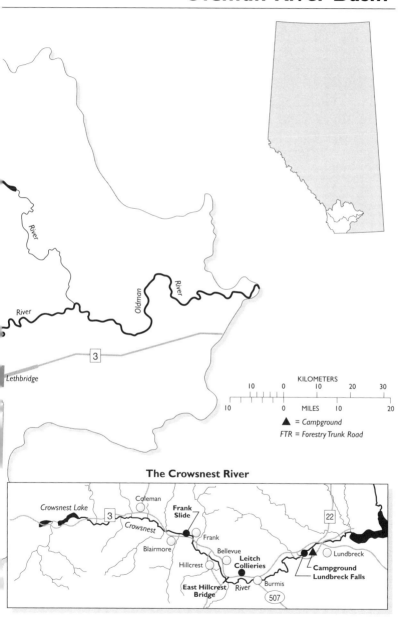

KILOMETERS

10   0   10   20   30

10   0   MILES   10   20

▲ = Campground
FTR = Forestry Trunk Road

The Crowsnest River

The Oldman reservoir was created in the early 1990s with the construction of an irrigation storage dam on the mainstem of the Oldman River a short distance below the confluence of the Oldman, Castle and Crowsnest rivers. The dam turned twenty-eight miles of the rivers into a giant, three-toed reservoir.

With the completion of this dam many trout fishers, including this one, were angered at the loss of huge portions of Alberta's best trout streams. Some consolation was the hope that a good tailwater fishery might develop in the Oldman below the dam. A tailwater fishery is one that develops downstream of a bottom-draw dam. Because the water comes from the bottom of the reservoir, it is consistently cool, and coldwater trout habitat sometimes extends downstream farther than normal. It is too early to be sure, but as of this writing it appears that this might be happening.

The Oldman is a different river below the dam. The insect life is dense and more reminiscent of that in the Crowsnest than the upper Oldman. Hatches of Pale Morning Duns, Blue-winged Olives, midges and caddis are heavy and there are plenty of fourteen- to sixteen-inch rainbows and good-sized whitefish there to eat them.

But this is still a good news–bad news story. The good news is that the fishing is improving below the dam. The bad news is that just six miles below the dam, the river enters the Peigan Indian Reserve, where fishing is not permitted.

There are about twenty-five miles of the Oldman River inaccessible within the Peigan Reserve, and below there the river is somewhat of an unknown quantity. In the early 1990s brown trout were planted in this part of the river to kick start this part of the fishery, and these fish are beginning to turn up in anglers' catches. It is hoped that when this fishery matures it will provide good angling downstream as far as Lethbridge.

Downstream of Fort Macleod two major tributaries, the Waterton and St. Mary rivers, join the Oldman from the south. The Waterton begins on the Alberta–Montana border in Waterton Lakes National Park and flows northward through the Waterton Reservoir before joining the Oldman west of Lethbridge. The Waterton has good fishing for browns, rainbows, cutthroats and whitefish with the best fishing found between Waterton Lakes and the reservoir.

A major tributary to the Waterton is the Belly River, which rises in Montana and flows north, joining the Waterton south of Fort Macleod. Though it carries a substantial variety of fish—rainbows, bull trout, cutthroats and whitefish—they are generally small and it is not regarded as highly as the Waterton. Its main claim to fame is that it occasionally produces an arctic grayling that has moved down from Lake Elizabeth in Montana.

The St. Mary River is the easternmost trout-producing tributary of the Oldman, rising in Montana, flowing north past the town of Cardston, through the St. Mary Reservoir and on to join the Oldman near Lethbridge. It carries rainbows, cutthroats and whitefish.

Aside from the major tributaries there are dozens of beautiful small creeks in the Oldman system. Streams like Racehorse, Dutch, Pincher, Gold and upper Willow creeks are beautiful places to fish and even better places to teach children to fish. The trout are small but willing, just like the kids trying to catch them.

The upper portions of most streams in the system have sparse hatches. The most important insects are the Western Green Drake mayfly and the golden stonefly, both of which hatch in midsummer. There are other flies also, of course, including Pale Morning Duns and caddis. Both the intensity of the hatches and the need for more sophisticated fly patterns and angling techniques increase as you move downstream.

THE GREAT WATERS: *The Crowsnest River*

If you could design your own trout stream you'd probably make it big enough to hold large trout but small enough to wade across. You'd be sure to include choppy broken water, long pools, dancing riffles and glassy slicks. You'd want some meadow water as well as some forested sections. There would have to be lots of bugs to feed lots of fish and maybe a salmonfly hatch for extra excitement. And as long as you were at it you could throw in some beautiful mountain scenery. Well, you don't need those blueprints. God beat you to it when He put this perfect trout stream in Alberta, and it's considered the best trout stream in the Oldman River system.

I first fished the Crowsnest River in 1982, so I can hardly claim old-timer's status there. In my early years on the Crow the river was not yet famous, and fishing it carried a certain sense of exploration. I caught some nice fish back then, but the most memorable one was a big rainbow I found below Lundbreck Falls in June of 1983.

I was showing off the river (what little I knew about it) to Richard Beeken from Edmonton, who a few years prior had guided with me on the Bow River. We caught some sizable fish in the Crow, but one afternoon below the stone house that sits at the confluence of Todd Creek I hooked a truly big fish. Richard watched me from the next pool upstream as I chased the trout downriver and back and forth before finally landing it. It was a twenty-three-inch rainbow that remained my biggest Crowsnest fish for the better part of a decade.

Now fast-forward to the spring of 1991 when some friends and I are trying to make a fly-fishing video. Things aren't exactly hunky dory. The water is high, we've had more technical problems than Apollo 13 and everyone is a little frustrated.

The middle section of the Crowsnest River.

Not much has gone right, but finally, in the same choppy pool that had given me the big rainbow so many years earlier, I hook a serious fish with the camera rolling. The trout takes a nymph in shallow water and races downriver, running and jumping and making me nervous. I land him for the camera and then release him, and it is not until later, after the excitement has died down, that déjà vu sets in. But for the passage of eight years this might be the same trout. It is a twenty-three-inch rainbow, and it has come from beside the same rock in the same pool. I don't know what this means, but I do know it will not happen a third time, for this lovely pool now sleeps beneath the water of the Oldman Reservoir.

Since then my movie career has, shall we say, cooled off somewhat, but the fishing on the Crowsnest River has not. In fact it has improved. Fish of this size are still not routine, but they are more common than they used to be, and fish in the fifteen- to nineteen-inch range are now very plentiful.

It is variety that draws me to this stream. There are times when size 2 stonefly nymphs on a 7-weight outfit are the perfect medicine; there are other times when size 22 midges on 6x tippets are the *only* medicine. There is great streamer fishing, and there is the bank a friend showed me where twenty-inch fish regularly sip dries from six inches of water.

The river drains Crowsnest Lake near the British Columbia border and weaves its way past Crowsnest Mountain, then through the tired coal-mining towns of Coleman, Blairmore, Frank and Bellevue before dropping over Lundbreck Falls. From the falls the river flows five miles east before entering the Oldman reservoir. All told there are nearly thirty miles of wonderful trout water on this river.

The upper river above Blairmore glides through beautiful alpine meadows with stable grassy banks and lovely smooth flows. The fish are primarily rainbows and whitefish with the occasional cutthroat. They are generally but not exclusively small.

Below Blairmore is a short stretch of still water created when the Frank Slide temporarily blocked the river. Float tubers sometimes work this water, seeking the enormous fish that appear to cruise briefly and then vanish into crevices between Turtle Mountain boulders the size of large cars.

The most popular water is between the town of Bellevue and Lundbreck Falls. The river here is in an enclosed valley, heavily timbered and rich with the scent of evergreen, aspen and willow. It is quite literally full of rainbow trout and whitefish.

From Lundbreck Falls to the reservoir, the river is different —wider, more open and hence more exposed to the Crowsnest Pass wind that permanently shapes the trees here. Below the falls the fish are still primarily rainbows and whitefish, but they share the rocky runs with some big browns and bull trout. In May enormous rainbows move out of the reservoir to spawn in the river.

One of the reasons for the Crowsnest's productivity is the abundance and diversity of insect life that thrives and feeds the fish. Hatch-chasing season usually begins with the appearance of Blue-winged Olives and midges in April and then March Brown mayflies in May. The fishing before runoff can be very good under low, clear water conditions, but this is also spawning season and anglers must be careful not to disturb the spawning fish or wade through the redds where their eggs have been laid. The redds are oval-shaped depressions in the gravel and are easy to recognize because the disturbed gravel is a lighter color than the surrounding area. Fish often build redds in the shallow tailouts of pools—just the kinds of places you'd probably choose to cross the river.

The last week of May is circled on many anglers' calendars, for that is when the Crowsnest's salmonflies begin to hatch. Salmonflies are two-inch-long stoneflies named for the orange color of their thoraxes. These creatures crawl out from under rocks in the river and migrate to the banks before emerging on dry land. The hatch starts on the lower river in late May and gradually progresses upstream, taking about two weeks to reach Blairmore.

On the Crowsnest, as elsewhere, this hatch often coincides with spring runoff and becomes little more than an interesting but academic entry in the fishing diary: "Great hatch, but water three feet high and muddy; couldn't fish."

When the water is fishable I've had wonderful nymphing before, during and after the salmonfly hatch with a big Bitch Creek or Poly Stone Nymph. As long as there are two feet or more of visibility in the water, the fish have no trouble finding the big, black nymphs.

It sometimes takes a couple of weeks of salmonfly activity before the dry-fly fishing gets rolling. By then the fish have had a chance to see and eat some adult flies that have fallen in or returned to the water to lay eggs. The best dries are orange-bodied Letort Hoppers or Stimulators in size 4 and 6.

A week or two after the salmonflies hatch, the slightly smaller golden stoneflies take their turn, and both fish and anglers get excited all over again.

Through the summer the Crowsnest River becomes a hatch-matcher's dream. Green Drakes, caddis, Pale Morning Duns, midges and numerous small stoneflies hatch, and the fish like them all. The dream can occasionally become a nightmare though, for these fish seem to delight in choosing the smallest flies and eating them in hilariously difficult spots: in the reverse flows of foamy back eddies or way back under overhanging alder bushes. As on most Alberta waters, late season on the Crowsnest is dominated by the extremes—huge hoppers and micromatches of Blue-winged Olives and midges.

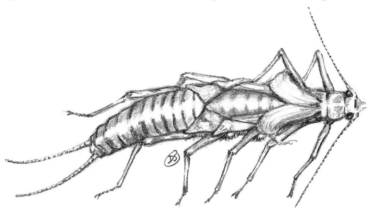

Emerging Stonefly

Though I now know the Crowsnest as a fine dry-fly stream, what initially drew me to it was the outstanding nymph-fishing it provides. From heavy dredging with giant stoneflies in early season to "far and fine" nymphing with size 18 Pheasant Tails in the fall, I know of no better nymph-fishing classroom than this stream. Along with rainbows the river is loaded with whitefish, and many of southern Alberta's best nymph-fishers cut their teeth on the "wiley whities" of the Crowsnest River.

Most nymph-fishers today use a floating fly line, a conventional nine-foot tapered leader with a brightly colored strike indicator and often some additional weight attached to the leader. The distance between the fly and the indicator should equal about twice the depth of the water.

Productive nymphing is usually a short-range game. Except when fishing shallow flat water, it is best to keep the casts under thirty feet. Concentrate on areas of broken water and work along deflections, depressions, drop-offs and current seams. On the Crow pay particular attention to the heads of the pools where the riffles dump in. Let the fly drift naturally back toward you with the current, and when the indicator suggests something unusual has happened to your fly, set the hook to find out if you've got a rock or a trout.

A good rule in all fishing is to make it easy for the fish to take your fly. In nymph-fishing this means keeping your fly near the bottom of the stream, but to keep it there you'll need to adjust the amount of extra weight on the leader or the distance between the indicator and the fly. How do you know if the fly is getting deep enough? By noticing how often it gets snagged on the stream bottom. If it never happens, you need more weight on the leader. If it happens nearly every cast, you need less weight. If it happens occasionally, your setup is probably just right. Human nature will tempt you to resist making these adjustments, but failing to make them is the single biggest mistake people make in nymph-fishing.

The Crowsnest is a good place to fish two nymphs simultaneously. The second one can be attached to a dropper on the leader, but I prefer to simply join the two flies with a separate piece of tippet and then tie one of them to the leader. If extra weight is needed it can be attached to the leader above the upper fly or between the two flies. I seem to get fewer horrendous tangles when I fish two flies this way, and if I want to change to a streamer or dry I can remove both nymphs by untying only one knot.

If I had a secret technique on the Crow it would be streamer-fishing. Streamers are the most overlooked tool on the river, and they work very well, especially when the water is a little high and a little off-color. I've taken some nice rainbows and a couple of huge browns on small Wooly Buggers, Spring Creek Buggers and Clouser Minnows.

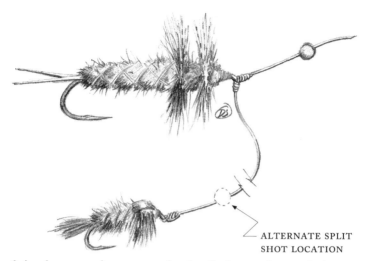

*A simple way to rig two nymphs. A split shot can be attached
between the two flies or 6 – 12 inches above the upper one. The two
flies should be 12 – 16 inches apart.*

The Crowsnest River we fish today does not flow quite as
Na'pi originally planned. When the irrigation dam and reservoir were built on the mainstem Oldman River, amidst much
opposition and controversy, nearly thirty miles of flowing water
were stilled. In order to compensate for the loss of moving
water habitat, the provincial government undertook a "mitiga-
tion" project to improve the fish-holding capability on the
portions of the rivers that remained. The greatest concentration of this work took place on the Crowsnest River downstream of Lundbreck Falls.

You can see much of this work from the gravel road that
parallels the lower river. Each time I stop the truck and look
down from the road at the twenty-four rock structures in the
Horseshoe Bend, I'm stricken by the artificiality of it all, and I
can't help thinking they overdid it. But when I'm standing
down in one of those man-made pools, catching more fish

than I deserve, my vision narrows until I see nothing but trout, and my opinion softens a little.

If I had to find something bad to say about this river it would be that it seems too many people are fishing it. The Crowsnest has become very famous and is often crowded on summer weekends. No doubt I must take a share of the blame for this, but with the river's fame has come special recognition and special regulations to protect the fishery, and it's a trade-off I think I can live with.

The increase in pressure has come largely from serious fly-fishers who catch the fish but do not take them home. This has little biological effect on the trout if they're handled properly, but when they are caught and released they become more difficult to catch the next time. I expect this trend to continue and note that the Crowsnest is already becoming a more "technical" stream often requiring fine leaders and very small flies to fool the fish.

Strangely enough the most crowded time on the river might be February and March. Much of the river is still frozen over then, but springs keep a small portion of it open below Bellevue. When a Chinook weather system arrives on a Friday afternoon and warms everything up, weekend anglers from Lethbridge and Calgary head for the Crow and participate in an unplanned anglers' gathering in the open water below the Leitch Collieries.

The upper portion of river above the East Hillcrest bridge is currently closed from November 1 to May 31, and a small section of prime spawning water between Lundbreck Falls and the Highway 3 bridge downstream is closed from April 1 to June 15. A slot limit, protecting trout between twelve and eighteen inches, is in effect in the water downstream of the East Hillcrest bridge. It appears that provincial officials are still tuning the regulations on this river, and more changes in the future will not be a surprise.

The Oldman is a river system whose reputation has been built on one stream: the Crowsnest River. But as Vic Bergman points out in his video *Fly Fishing Alberta's Chinook Country,* there are dozens of streams worth fishing in this corner of Alberta. And if the Crowsnest River is now being loved a little too hard by all its friends, my hope is that other streams in the area will take some of the pressure off it as their quality is recognized. When you go to fish the Crowsnest, do yourself a favor and explore a few of the other great streams that are nearby too. Na'pi would like that.

Access and Accommodation

Access to the upper Oldman and Livingstone rivers and their tributaries is provided by the Forestry Trunk Road. Highways 517 and 22 provide access to the Oldman itself.

The Oldman Dam is accessible on secondary roads north of Highway 3. There is a four-mile float from the dam to the Summerview bridge, but most anglers elect to fish this on foot. The Cottonwood Campground just below the dam was washed out in the flood of June 1995 but will be rebuilt. The river below the Peigan Reserve is accessible from Highway 2 or the town of Fort Macleod.

The Crowsnest is a very accessible river. Highway 3 follows its valley west to the British Columbia border, and numerous side roads and secondary highways cross it. Good maps of access sites are available from fly shops in the Crowsnest Pass and in Calgary.

Highway 507 and secondary roads off it provide access to

the Castle River and Highway 774 provides access to the West Castle.

The Waterton River is accessible from Highway 6 and secondary roads off it, and both the Waterton and Belly rivers are accessible from Highway 505.

The St. Mary is accessible from Cardston and the city of Lethbridge.

Motel accommodation is available in the towns of Pincher Creek, Blairmore, Fort McLeod, Lethbridge and Cardston, and Bed and Breakfasts are very common throughout the Crowsnest Pass. There are also numerous campgrounds on Highway 3, the Forestry Trunk Road and secondary roads in the area.

Hatch Chart

Date	*Hatch*	*Imitation*
April 15 – May 15	Blue-winged Olive	Adams, Crystal Blue-winged Olive, size 18, 20
May 15 – June 15	March Brown	Adams, Quad March Brown, size 14
May 20 – Aug 30	Caddis	Elk Hair Caddis, size 12 – 18
May 25 – June 25	Salmonfly	Orange Stimulator, size 4 – 8

June 10 – July 15	Golden stonefly	Yellow Stimulator, size 6 – 10
June 15 – July 20	Pale Morning Dun	Pale Morning Dun Parachute, size 16
June 20 – July 20	Western Green Drake	Olive Paradrake, Crystal Green Drake, size 8, 10
July 15 – Aug 15	Small Western Green Drake	Olive Humpy, Crystal Green Drake, size 12
July 20 – Sept 15	Grasshopper	Hopper-cator, Dave's Hopper, size 6 – 12
Aug 15 – Sept 15	Fall Caddis	Orange Stimulator, size 6, 8
Sept 1 – Oct 15	Blue-winged Olive	Adams, Crystal Blue-winged Olive, size 18, 20

7

The BOW RIVER SYSTEM

I N LATE AUGUST OF 1995 I floated a portion of the Bow River downstream of Calgary as I have done over four hundred times in the last twenty years. My companion was Jim Gilson from central Pennsylvania, who was concluding his seventeenth trip to the Bow. We were hoping for a spectacular day of fishing to finish Jim's trip, but in truth nothing out of the ordinary happened, and the day had a decidedly average flavor to it. The trout showed great disdain for the hoppers we cast from the drifting boat, so we had to get out and work the water with nymphs to catch fish. The action was never furious, but we picked up a fish here and there on nymphs and then a few on streamers. Later on we found some fish rising to the afternoon *Baetis* hatch, and we caught a couple of nice rainbows on small dry flies.

When we pulled the boat out of the river at dark we were a little disappointed at the ordinariness of our day. Then on the way home one of us—I don't remember who—started to laugh out loud: "Hold on a minute. Let's pretend we were on another river—the Henry's Fork, Beaverkill, Madison. How would we feel if we'd had this day on one of those rivers?"

The answer was clear. On nearly any other river in North

America, hooking twenty fish and landing six or eight over twenty-inches long would be cause for celebration or at least a phone call to the local fly shop to brag. But on the Bow we were disappointed. That seems to summarize the reputation of this river. It is judged on a different set of criteria than nearly all other trout streams, even the great ones. Certainly the Bow River experience can be as much exasperation as exhilaration, particularly for an inexperienced angler, but when it is cooperating even a little, the Bow is simply beyond compare.

Early last summer I had an evening that reminded me of this. I spent a couple of hours walking the river, looking for "snouts"—the gentle rises of fish feeding in shallow water along the banks. But snout hunting is an inexact science; sometimes I find them and sometimes I don't.

This night I found them, and each was a big, hard rainbow, supercharged the way only Bow River fish can be. Four times my reel was emptied of line by trout I had to chase down the river to land. The biggest weighed close to five pounds, and several were simply too hot to handle on 5x tippet and size 16 dry flies.

THE BIG PICTURE

From source to mouth the Bow River passes through three distinct geographic zones: the Rocky Mountains, the foothills and the prairie. Along the way are bighorn sheep, moose, bears, canoeists, fly-fishers, mountain climbers, busloads of tourists, the Olympic Ski Jump, the Calgary Tower, mule deer, mule deer hunters, antelope and rattlesnakes. It is nearly four hundred miles from Bow Lake in Banff National Park to the Grand Forks, where the Bow meets the Oldman in the shortgrass prairie west of the city of Medicine Hat.

There are places where the long history of human settlement in the Bow corridor is painfully obvious, the city of Calgary being just one example. Yet there are also places on the river where months might pass between human visits. The upper portion of the river, which flows through today's Banff National Park, was initially occupied by the Stoney Indians and then by the early white explorers seeking a route through the Rockies. The Bow Basin was regarded as a frontier of one type or another for over a hundred years as first the fur trade and then railroad construction, law enforcement and eventually the oil industry drew people to seek their fortune in the mountains and foothills of what was to become southern Alberta.

The Bow River begins like many other western rivers as a tiny gathering of snowmelt in the high country of the Rocky Mountains. Nothing in its infancy is unusual; nothing hints of the fame it will achieve later.

The Bow River system drains 9,800 square miles and receives help in this task from upper tributaries like the Kananaskis, Spray and Ghost rivers, which meet the Bow in the mountains and foothills. The Elbow River is a major tributary that joins the Bow at Calgary, and the Highwood River meets the Bow in the middle of the "blue ribbon" section between Calgary and Carseland. From Calgary the Bow flows southeastward past the Bassano Dam and on to its confluence with the Oldman River in the desolate prairie south of the pheasant hunting center of Brooks. From this point on, the river is called the South Saskatchewan, which is then joined by the Red Deer River near Alberta's eastern boundary. Then, in the province of Saskatchewan, the South Saskatchewan River meets the North Saskatchewan River, and they become the Saskatchewan River (got that?). Thus all of Alberta's trout streams from the Athabasca south unite to flow into Hudson Bay.

Trout occupy approximately the upper two-thirds of the Bow River system though rainbows have been caught as much as one hundred miles below Calgary. The system contains three distinct fisheries: the Bow above Calgary, the tributaries and the Bow below Calgary.

The Bow Above Calgary

The best thing about the upper Bow River is that it is overshadowed by the river below Calgary. The whole fly-fishing world knows about the Calgary-to-Carseland stretch of the Bow, yet the upper river is still largely unknown. It receives little attention from anglers, and I'm tempted to say nothing about it to ensure it stays that way.

The dominant characteristic of the river here is its beautiful Rocky Mountain setting where wading anglers are distracted by panoramic views and must sometimes share the pools with thirsty Elk. From the headwaters near Bow Lake down to the town of Banff, the river is largely fast, clean and cold, and of more interest to white-water paddlers than fly-fishers. There are bull trout and cutthroats above Lake Louise, and brook trout become common between Lake Louise and Banff. The Bow's upper tributaries—creeks like Redearth, Johnston and Baker—carry small cutthroats. The upper Cascade River, which flows into the west end of Lake Minnewanka, carries a remarkable assortment of fish, including brook, rainbow, cutthroat and bull trout. It also boasts in its valley one of the heaviest concentrations of grizzly bears outside of Alaska.

In general the Bow and its tributaries above Banff lack many of the nutrients necessary to be highly productive trout streams. Though there are trout and whitefish here, these waters' biggest attraction lies in the wildness of the surroundings.

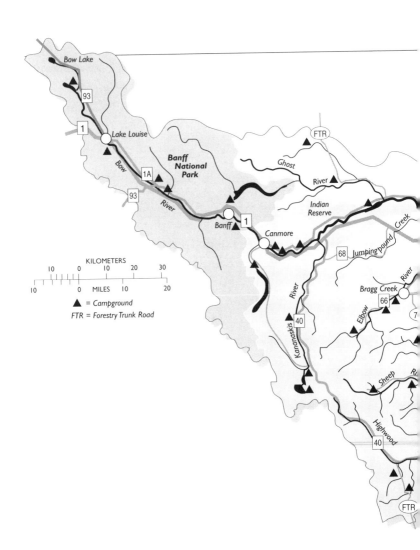

KILOMETERS

▲ = Campground
FTR = Forestry Trunk Road

Bow River Basin

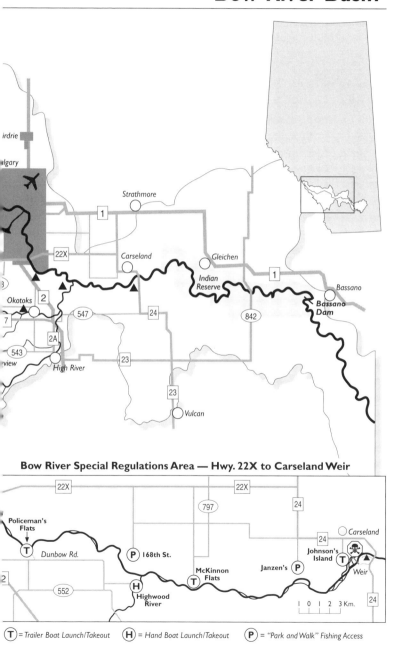

Strathmore

1

22X

Carseland

Gleichen

Indian
Reserve

1

Bassano

Bassano
Dam

842

irdrie

lgary

Okotoks 2

7

2A

543

view

547

24

23

23

High River

Vulcan

Bow River Special Regulations Area — Hwy. 22X to Carseland Weir

22X   22X

797   24

Policeman's
Flats

T   Dunbow Rd.   P 168th St.

McKinnon
Flats

24

Carseland

24

Johnson's
Island   T

Weir

Janzen's P

2   552

H
Highwood
River

T

24

| 0 | 2   3 Km.

(T) = Trailer Boat Launch/Takeout   (H) = Hand Boat Launch/Takeout   (P) = "Park and Walk" Fishing Access

The river between the town of Seebee and the Bearspaw Dam just west of Calgary is also relatively unproductive, but for a different reason. Three power dams in this section cause severe daily fluctuations in water level—bad news for any trout stream. Much of this water is also inaccessible because it lies within the Stoney Indian Reserve.

The best and most accessible fishing on the upper Bow, then, is in the thirty miles of river between the town of Banff and the first dam at Seebee. The river's productivity increases near the town of Banff because of the nutrients entering the river from both the town and the mineral-rich outflow of the Cave and Basin Hot Springs. The fish below Banff are brown trout that sometimes get big, brook trout that don't and white-fish that do and don't. Bull trout and cutthroats are present but relatively rare.

This beautiful water is sometimes floated by anglers in drift boats. The water is more demanding of an oarsman than that below Calgary, but it is within the range of someone with previous experience. It is generally best to keep to the main river channel as some of the smaller side channels have sweepers and log jams that can and do swamp boats.

Be aware that water conditions and even the river's actual path can change over time in the mountain regions. Always check the condition and safety of a particular stretch of water with the park information service in Banff or with an experienced floater before you float it for the first time. It is also wise to scout both put-in and take-out sites in advance of your trip.

Dan Bell, who guides fly-fishers on the upper Bow, reports that streamers are very reliable here. He prefers dark patterns like olive or black Crystal Buggers on cloudy days and white ones on sunny days. Nymphs also work well, and the fish often show a preference for the Gold Ribbed Hare's Ear in olive.

Many fly-fishers consider the upper Bow to be great dry-fly water except during spring runoff, which begins in late May and lasts for one to two weeks. Floating and fishing the river at this time of high water are both poor ideas. The prime dry-fly season usually begins with the appearance of the golden stoneflies in early July. The Stimulator in size 6 or 8 is a good imitation of this big clumsy bug. Both golden stones and juicy Western Green Drake mayflies provide good fishing through August. There are caddisflies around throughout the summer and fall, too, including at least one species that dives into the water to lay eggs. Consequently a sparsely dressed Elk Hair Caddis fished under the surface can work very well at times. There are also minor hatches of Pale Morning Duns, and good late-summer hatches of Blue-winged Olives and Red Quills. Attractor dries like Wulffs and Trudes are good bets when the fish aren't rising. The fishing usually holds up well through September, but late fall is often disappointing because a very high percentage of the adult brown trout move into small tributaries to spawn.

Be aware that a portion of the upper Bow lies within Banff National Park and that a parks fishing license is required to fish the river there. Also be aware that the regulations are different in the park, and as of this writing, fishing is not allowed between two hours after sunset and one hour before sunrise. Also, Bow tributaries in the park are open to angling only in July and August, and the regulations forbid the killing of any bull trout or cutthroats.

Bow Tributaries

In this watershed, unlike the Red Deer and North Saskatchewan, it is the main river that holds the greatest attraction to fly-fishers seeking larger trout. With some exceptions the tributaries' main role is to provide spawning and rearing water for the trout that live in the main river. Consequently the tributaries carry primarily, though not exclusively, smaller fish. The largest fish in the tributaries are often bull trout.

The first major stream to join the Bow outside Banff National Park is the Kananaskis River, which meets the Bow downstream of Canmore. Many anglers salivate and get hot flushes when they first see this river from the Trans-Canada Highway, for its beautiful pools are clear and inviting. And the Kananaskis was once a fine trout stream, but it is now a reluctant impostor. The fluctuations in water level caused by the three power dams upstream have virtually ruined it as a trout fishery.

The Ghost River joins the Bow from the north, flowing into the Ghost Reservoir, an impoundment on the Bow created by the Ghost Dam. It is a small gravelly stream lacking some of the nutrients and overwintering water that a first-class stream requires.

One of the best Bow tributaries is Jumping Pound Creek, which joins the river from the south at Cochrane. It carries a healthy population of resident rainbows and also serves as an important spawning stream for rainbows coming out of the Bearspaw Reservoir each spring. Unfortunately the lower reaches of this stream flow through private land, where public access is severely restricted. The upper portions, though, are accessible from Highway 68. A Jumping Pound tributary, Sibbald Creek, has a good set of beaver ponds on it.

The Elbow River joins the Bow in the city of Calgary, and it is an underrated and underfished stream. In the city, below the Glenmore Dam, the Elbow has resident brown trout and whitefish, and the fishing can be quite good if you happen to be there when the water level is suitable. The Glenmore

Reservoir is a water source for the city of Calgary, so a high volume of water is maintained in the reservoir, which means inconsistent flows in the river below. The Elbow below Glenmore Dam is frequently either nearly in flood or nearly dried up.

Above Calgary the Elbow River carries all our cold-water fish except grayling. It produces some nice cutthroats, a few good browns and the occasional huge bull trout.

The Highwood River is the last major tributary to join the Bow, doing so about fifteen miles downstream of Calgary. The Highwood system is an important fishery in southern Alberta. It carries resident rainbows, cutthroats and mountain whitefish, and fair numbers of bull trout. Rainbows from the Bow below Calgary spawn in the streams in the Highwood system each spring, and consequently the entire system is closed to angling during this period.

The upper Highwood system, from the town of Longview west, is one of the most beautiful places in Alberta to cast a fly. The oil wells and cattle ranches that have dominated this landscape of sky, evergreens and grass are now sharing it with Hollywood moviemakers. A number of major films have been shot in the area, including Clint Eastwood's *Unforgiven*. The Highwood has a number of tributaries worth fishing, including the Sheep River and smaller streams like Pekisko, Ware, Three Point, Trap and Cataract creeks.

Insect hatches throughout the upper Highwood system are typical of the high country: sparse, diverse and requiring little in the way of precise hatch-matching. After runoff, which begins in mid- to late May and usually lasts for a couple of weeks, attractor dry flies are the order of the day. These streams are particularly fine places for new anglers to hone their skills.

The lower Highwood and its tributaries have sparse versions of the same hatches we see on the Bow below Calgary. The fish are generally small, but occasionally you'll be surprised by a big rainbow from the Bow that has taken up residence after spawning. The lower Highwood and Sheep rivers also host a huge run of whitefish that move up from the Bow to spawn each fall.

Anglers are advised to check the fishing regulations carefully before striking out in the Bow system. The rules regarding seasons, limits and the use of bait are not the same on all streams or even on all parts of the Bow proper.

The Great Waters: *The Bow Below Calgary*

The stately prairie river that weaves its way from the city limits of Calgary to the town of Carseland is probably Canada's most famous trout stream. Each year anglers from the United States, Japan and Europe come to Alberta not to see West Edmonton Mall or the Calgary Stampede but rather to fish this part of the Bow.

The benchmark for bragging-sized trout in North American streams is twenty inches. On most streams, twenty-inchers are rare or nonexistent; on a few streams they are occasional, pleasant surprises. On the Bow below Calgary, they are expected. The size of its fish has been perhaps the only constant on this river known for its great unpredictability. The Bow below Calgary is today, and has been for the twenty-five years I have fished it, a river that produces larger average trout than virtually any other stream in North America. It continues to give capable fly-fishers many, many trout between twenty and twenty-four inches long.

This fishery developed through a fortunate yet unplanned interaction of natural and artificial factors. On the natural side the river in the Calgary area possesses a number of desirable "trouty" qualities. The structure of the river bed and the speed, depth and temperature of the water create ideal trout habitat. In addition, both rainbows and browns have access to good spawning water.

On the artificial side are two major factors. One is the Bearspaw Dam, which was built on the Bow just upstream of Calgary in 1954. Its purpose is to prevent flooding in low-lying areas of the city by stabilizing the erratic flow rates caused by several power dams upstream, but the trout also benefit from this restored stability. The other factor is the release of phosphates and nitrates into the Bow by the city of Calgary. This stimulates plant growth, which provides habitat for the aquatic insects and other organisms that trout eat. So ideally yet accidentally we have a rich, relatively stable river with great trout habitat, abundant food and suitable spawning water.

Of course it's not quite that simple because the Bow is not a static system. The steady growth of the city of Calgary has occasionally resulted in too much phosphate and nitrate being released into the river. Many times through the second half of this century the city has had to improve its waste-water treatment facilities to meet the demands of its increasing population. These improvements have typically occurred just in time to prevent serious dissolved oxygen problems from developing in the river.

It's also fortunate that the Bow carries both rainbow and brown trout, not only because they are the hardiest species of trout but also because they spawn in opposite seasons. The rainbows spawn in the spring when flooding in the small tributaries can sometimes damage the eggs and fry while the browns spawn in the more stable autumn. It is unlikely that both species would have poor recruitment the same year. Consequently the proportion of browns to rainbows shifts from year to year as one species outspawns the other.

While this part of the Bow undoubtedly produces more big trout than any moving water in Alberta, it is also a most difficult piece of water to get to know. Anglers new to fly-fishing as well as experienced fly-fishers new to this river are often—no, *usually* —frustrated by this stream, at least for a while. They hear all the reports, see all the videos and still have all kinds of trouble.

The main difficulty is the size of the river. Often a hundred yards wide, its sheer volume of water puts many people off their game. I often encourage new anglers to focus on smaller side channels created by numerous islands in the river to help reduce this intimidation factor.

The increased pressure on the Bow in recent years also has contributed to anglers' problems: It has made the fish more difficult to catch. Today's consistently successful Bow River anglers have become versatile by necessity. They fish with a variety of methods, changing them frequently and letting the fish decide which one is most effective.

The most reliable way to catch fish on the Bow below Calgary is with nymphs, and one of the best flies for this method is the one euphemistically called the "thin red nymph." It's the San Juan Worm, an imitation of the aquatic worm that lives in the weeds of the river. Other good choices are standard and revised versions of the Gold Ribbed Hare's Ear, Pheasant Tail and Prince Nymph in sizes 8 through 14. European bead head-style nymphs arrived in North America in 1992 and are now very popular on the Bow. While nymphs can be used successfully from a drifting boat, I prefer to fish them while wading. The methods outlined in Chapter Six work on the Bow, though it is a more difficult stream to read. It is best to concentrate on the deflections and depressions in broken water near the banks.

Except in late-summer hopper season, the dry-fly fishing on this part of the Bow requires rising fish, and finding them on a big river is a skill that requires practice. The fish like to rise in shallow, slow water near the banks of the river, often in the tailouts of huge pools or on the inside of large bends. They don't like to do it in direct sunshine, so on bright days look for them on the shady side of the river working quietly in the deflections along the banks. The biggest fish often make the smallest rises, so look for gentle dimples rather than showy splashes.

The first fly to get fish looking up is a midday caddis that begins to hatch in May. Then in June, Pale Morning Dun mayflies start to emerge and are soon joined by blizzards of evening caddis that produce the late-day dry-fly fishing for which the river is famous.

By early August the tiny white-winged, black-bodied *Tricorythodes* mayfly spinners are swarming each morning. This bug now has the dubious reputation of being our most visible yet unproductive hatch. Fish still feed on tricos, I'm sure, but the activity is erratic, unpredictable and short-lived, and few anglers pursue it.

Perhaps the mayfly the fish rise to best is the Blue-winged Olive, which begins hatching in August and continues through mid-October. This bug emerges heaviest on dreary, dark September days, and my standard advice to visiting autumn anglers is *not* to stay inside if it looks like it might rain.

Another very important insect on the Bow is the golden stonefly—likely one or more of the *Acroneuria* species—and though it doesn't provide dry-fly fishing the way some of the caddis and mayflies do, the nymphs are present in the river in good numbers all the time. A golden stone nymph like the Magic Stone or Pennstone in size 6 or 8 is never a bad choice.

Beginning in late July big fish can regularly be taken by drifting hoppers along the banks of the river. In early August you might use a size 12 fly, but by mid-September the natural hoppers will be bigger, and you might step your imitation up to a size 6 or 8.

A clever way to fish two flies has become popular on the Bow in recent years. A high-floating hopper or Stimulator dry fly is tied to the leader, and a small bead head nymph is attached to a dropper about eighteen inches long. The dry fly functions as both fly and indicator for the nymph. This "hopper-dropper" rig is especially effective when cast from a drifting boat.

The Hopper-dropper rig. A buoyant dry fly is fished together with a nymph. The two flies should be 1 – 2 feet apart.

Streamers also are an important tool on the Bow, but in my recent experience they are inconsistent. Some days the fish can't stay away from them and other days they stay away in droves. I have not figured out who or what turns the switch.

Streamers are commonly fished in two ways. The first is from a drifting boat with a floating or sink-tip line. The rower positions the boat a comfortable distance from the bank, and the angler casts into the holding water along the banks and retrieves the fly back to the boat. Streamers can also be fished from your feet, in which case a sink-tip line is best. The cast is made across and downstream, and the fly is allowed to swing through the likely lies before being retrieved.

In order to achieve the versatility required on the Bow, an angler needs either one all-round outfit like a 9-foot, 6-weight rod, or two outfits—a 7- or 8-weight for streamers and a 4- or 5-weight for dries and nymphs.

The Bow below Calgary typically undergoes a spring runoff beginning near the end of May that renders the river unfishable for a period of one to three weeks. There are also times in early summer when the Bow itself is clear, but the Highwood River is still dirty from rain or runoff. Anglers are then advised to fish the Bow above its confluence with the Highwood.

Anglers should also be aware that heavy rain in Calgary can turn the river dirty very suddenly. The rainwater runs quickly from the pavement through the storm sewer system into the river. The bad news is that it is futile to try to fish in these conditions. The good news is that once the rain stops and the streets are dry the river clears again almost immediately. It can go from completely clear to completely muddy and back again in twenty-four hours.

Much of the Bow stays open all winter in and below Calgary for some distance, and fishing during a period of warm Chinook weather certainly beats watching TV. The fishing from November through March is almost entirely a wet-fly game with nymphs, streamers and leech patterns being the most effective flies. The cold water slows the fish's metabolism, and winter anglers must fish slow, deep pools with slow, deep methods.

The portion of the river from the Highway 22X bridge to the Carseland irrigation weir is regulated differently than the rest of the river: Fishing is open all year, bait is not allowed, there is no-kill during April and May, and a limit of two trout under sixteen inches the rest of the year. Check current regulations for details and possible changes. Note also that fishing is not permitted from the west bank of the river within the Inglewood Bird Sanctuary downstream of 17th Avenue in Calgary.

There is a widely held view that it is impossible to fish below Calgary without a boat. This is incorrect and unfortunate. There are a number of public access sites in and below the city, where good fishing is available to those who don't mind walking a few minutes to get away from the majority of other anglers. Having said that, I'll add that few western rivers are more suited to floating than the Bow in and below Calgary. The water is easily navigable in a number of different crafts. Vehicle shuttle service is available for floaters and can be arranged through fly shops in Calgary.

Though the famous portion of the Bow is between Calgary and Carseland, the good fishing doesn't abruptly stop at the Carseland irrigation weir. There is exceptionally fine water down to and through the Blackfoot Indian Reserve below Carseland. What does stop abruptly is easy access to the river. In the past, fishing permits and information on access have been available from the Blackfoot band, but the band's policy on sport-fishing has not always been clear or permanent. A call to the Blackfoot office in the town of Gleichen is the first step in arranging to fish this reach of the Bow on your own. A number of outfitters have explored this water, but Eric Grinnell's Silvertip Outfitters has been fishing below Carseland almost exclusively for many years.

In spite of my efforts here, many anglers will continue to struggle with the Bow below Calgary, particularly if they fish it alone. I know of no other stream where up-to-date local help is so necessary. The best advice I can give is to get some of this help through Calgary fly shops or the Hook and Hackle Club. Talk to a friend who knows the river or hire a guide for a day or two. It is also important to persist. The learning curve is very gentle initially, and there are no shortcuts, but this piece of water is well worth the time it takes to get to know it.

Local anglers have known something interesting was going on in the Bow River since the 1940s, but the word really got out internationally in the early 1980s, when feature stories about the Bow began turning up in prominent American outdoor magazines. The authors were different, but the stories were the same—rave reviews about a lightly fished river where huge trout fed on the surface all day long. "The best dry-fly stream in the world" were the words used by renowned fly-fisherman Lefty Kreh.

Through the 1980s the Bow enjoyed great fame as a dry-fly river. After that its reputation began to slip. Some regular visitors stopped coming, some local anglers gave up on it and a common question was "What's happened to the Bow?" What happened was that many of the fish quit feeding on the surface. It was still possible to take plenty of big trout on sinking flies, but many anglers accustomed to the earlier dry-fly action or tuned to expect it by the magazine articles were disappointed. Explanations were needed, and anglers obliged with numerous theories.

Some people thought the fish were rising less because of reduced weed growth in the river after the city upgraded its phosphate removal equipment. Others felt that erratic water levels brought on by unusual weather patterns through the late 1980s and early 1990s caused the changes in the trout's feeding behavior. This was my favorite theory, and I expounded on it in somewhat convoluted detail in the 1989 book *Fish & Tell & Go To Hell.* A more contentious opinion, which even made it to the pages of *Fly Fisherman* magazine, was that an increased number of white pelicans were eating the rising trout or at least convincing them that rising was not a good idea. We were quite pleased with all these theories, for they made for interesting conversation and held up quite nicely until the summer of 1995.

In June of that year a violent storm, which coincided precisely with the beginning of spring runoff, dropped six to ten inches of rain on southern Alberta in twenty-four hours. Some rivers like the Oldman and Highwood reached flood levels not seen this century. Virtually every trout stream in southern Alberta, including the Bow, was severely scoured and substantially changed.

We feared the worst for our trout streams, but on the Bow below Calgary what emerged from the silty floodwaters was a rejuvenated dry-fly river. When it cleared and became fishable in late July, we had the best dry-fly fishing of the last ten years. So how about all those great theories? Well, if you'll pardon the expression, they don't hold much water anymore. In 1995 there was virtually no weed growth in the river, the pelicans were still here and the spring weather was the worst anyone could remember. Unpredictable? You might say so.

Still, the river is different today than it was in the 1970s and 1980s, and perhaps the most noticeable difference is in the number of people fishing it. But is it crowded? That depends on your frame of reference. If you fished the river in the 1970s you'll notice a huge increase in the number of anglers on the river today. On the other hand, if you've just returned from sharing thirteen miles of water with one hundred other drift boats on the Bighorn River in Montana, you'll feel lonely on the Bow.

Another difference, and one I report with pleasure, is that there are more truly large fish being caught in the river now than at any time in memory. When I was guiding on the river in the late 1970s, fish over twenty-four inches long were very rare. Recently, though, there have been a surprising number of fish in the five- to eight-pound range caught each season. Nobody gets very many of these fish (I still don't get *any*), but about once a week now, somebody does.

The fishing in the Bow has changed over the last ten years, but I contend that we must expect such change because this river is subject not only to the natural influences that all trout streams face but also to a myriad of additional influences wrought through its bisection of 750,000 people. Different today? Most assuredly. Worse? Better? Yes, and yes.

The Bow is truly one of the great trout streams of the world, and every angler owes it to himself to try it. But be warned: It can quickly become an addiction. Perhaps the only bad part of the Bow River experience is that it causes some anglers to exclude other waters from their plans. As many Alberta fly-fishers put it, "Why would I go someplace else when I can fish the Bow?"

A section of the Bow between Calgary and Carseland—a big river with big fish.

Access and Accommodation

Foot access to the upper Bow is quite good. Between Exshaw and Lake Louise, Highway 1, 1A or both parallel the river extensively. Above Lake Louise access is available from Highway 93. There also is easy access to good water near the golf courses in both Banff and Canmore.

Though there are no actual boat ramps on the upper Bow, there are several places in this section where boat access is possible. The first is at the Bow's confluence with the Spray River in the town of Banff. The next is at the bridge in the town of Canmore, about fifteen miles and a full day's float from Banff. There also is access at the Highway 1 bridge just two and one-half miles and an easy evening's float downstream from the bridge in Canmore. A short distance below the Highway 1 bridge the main river channel is blocked by a massive log jam. Side channels can take you past this difficult spot, but local knowledge is essential to identifying the correct route. A float trip from this bridge is best done with people familiar with the problem and solution.

There is another access site at the Dead Man's Flats Campground on Highway 1, eight miles below the bridge, but it is an awkward take-out spot where the boat must be pulled up—believe it or not—a set of stairs.

The next access is off Highway 1A on the north side of the river at the town of Exshaw. The float from Dead Man's Flats to Exshaw is just four miles long, but much of it is through the slow water of Lac Des Arcs.

The final access site is at the bridge on the access road between Highways 1 and 1A, near the Kananaskis Guest Ranch, five miles below Exshaw. This area is known for the severe winds that often funnel through here on their way to the prairie.

As of this writing, there is no commercial shuttle service available on the upper Bow, so you must make your own arrangements or hire a cab in Canmore to help.

Hotel or motel accommodation is available in the towns of Canmore, Banff and Lake Louise. Campgrounds are abundant in Banff National Park, but both campgrounds and motels book up heavily in summer, so it is best to make reservations or to check in before noon.

Access and campground accommodation is available on the upper Highwood River from Highways 40 and 541, on the upper Elbow from Highway 66 and on the upper Sheep from Highway 546. The Sheep River also is accessible at Highway 2 and in the towns of Okotoks and Turner Valley. Note that Highway 40 is closed from the junction with Highway 541 to the northern boundary of Peter Lougheed Park between December 1 and June 15. This does not pose a problem to anglers as the streams are also closed to fishing then too.

The best access to the Elbow River above Calgary is near the town of Bragg Creek or upstream from there along Highway 66. Immediately west of Calgary the river is inaccessible because it flows through restricted military property and the Sarcee Indian Reserve.

On the middle or lower Bow, foot access is available throughout the city of Calgary and at a number of public boat launch and park-and-walk access sites between the city and Carseland. There is a boat launch site on the Bow in Calgary at the Cushing bridge on 17th Avenue, which is a safe distance downstream of a dangerous irrigation weir that must be avoided. Below there, boat access is available at Bonnybrook on Ogden Road, the Graves bridge on Glenmore Trail, the Highway 22x bridge, Policeman's Flats, McKinnon Flats and on the north bank at the Carseland weir. As of this writing there is some hope that additional ramps may soon be built at other sites, especially at the Ivor Strong bridge on Deerfoot Trail (between Glenmore Trail and Highway 22X).

People often ask how long it takes to make one of these floats. I usually avoid a direct answer, for the time it takes depends on a number of changing factors, including the time of year, the type of boat used and anglers' preference for floating or stopping and fishing. I consider a five-mile float good for a half-day or a whole day with plenty of stops, and I don't personally like floating more than fifteen miles in an entire day.

Most fly shops in Calgary can provide free maps of public access sites on the river, but the best map, produced as a fund-raiser by the Bow River Chapter of Trout Unlimited, includes hatch charts and other helpful information as well.

There are numerous motels and hotels in south Calgary, but there also is motel and bed-and-breakfast accommodation in the nearby towns of Okotoks and High River. There are a number of convenient campgrounds close to Calgary, including Pine Creek on Highway 2 just south of Calgary, Nature's Hideaway on the Highwood River just above its confluence with the Bow and on the Bow itself south of Carseland on Highway 24. There are also several campgrounds in Okotoks and High River.

Hatch Chart

Date	Hatch	Imitation
April 1 – May 15	Blue-winged Olive	Adams, Crystal Blue-winged Olive, size 18
May 15 – June 15	March Brown	Adams, Quad March Brown, size 14
May 20 – Aug 30	Caddis	Elk Hair Caddis, size 10 – 18
June 15 – July 20	Pale Morning Dun	Pale Morning Dun Parachute, size 16
June 15 – Aug 15	Golden Stonefly	Yellow Stimulator, size 6 – 10
July 15 – Aug 15	Western Green Drake	Olive Paradrake, Crystal Green Drake, size 8, 10
Aug 1 – Sept 20	Grasshopper	Dave's Hopper, Hopper-cator, size 6 – 12
Aug 1 – Sept 30	*Tricorythodes*	Trico Spinner, size 18, 20

| Aug 15 – Sept 15 | Fall Caddis | Orange Stimulator, size 6, 8 |
| Sept 1 – Oct 15 | Blue-winged Olive | Adams, Crystal Blue-winged Olive, size 18, 20 |

8

The RED DEER *and* NORTH SASKATCHEWAN RIVER SYSTEMS

O N A LATE SEPTEMBER DAY in 1974 my mind abandoned the University of Alberta lecture theater in search of water. I was trying to follow what the Ed. Psych. prof was saying, but it wasn't working, and before I knew it I had a plan: I'd bring my tackle with me the next morning, cut the afternoon classes and be on the stream by 3:00 P.M.

Shortly after noon the next day I pointed my Dad's old red pickup south on Highway 2, turned right at Innisfail, crossed the Red Deer and Medicine rivers and turned again onto gravel. It was a fine fall day in the western foothills. Frost had turned the aspens yellow, the sky was sapphire blue and everything was washed in the pure amber sunlight of an Alberta autumn. The little creek sang like a child while I put on waders and rigged a fly rod. On the water a few mayflies drifted among aspen leaves that had dropped from a tree leaning over the creek. Tight against the trunk of the tree was the occasional blip of a feeding brown trout.

This particular stream and this particular fish had been distracting me for weeks. I had seen and fished for the trout before, but without success. A friend who had showed me the spot and caught the fish, had named him the Tree Hole Trout.

I had even seen photographs of the fish, taken when my friend had caught and then released him.

It was a tricky place requiring a downstream cast from a kneeling position. A tall spruce stood right behind the only casting spot, and my first two attempts became two more donations to the tree's growing collection of flies that had formerly belonged to me. Eventually my Adams drifted nicely past the trunk of the tree. The fish ignored it and took another mayfly. The real flies looked pale, so I traded the somber Adams for a gingery Light Cahill. It bobbed along to the base of the tree and disappeared in the wet wink of a rise.

The fish jumped when he felt the hook, entering the September light and shattering the quietness of the moment. I fought and landed him from my knees and then took my own photograph of the Tree Hole Trout.

Then I did a most peculiar thing: I went home. I had driven over two hours to fish one pool, and having done that I was content. Nothing could have improved the moment, and for once I was smart enough to realize it.

In the years since, the leaning tree has fallen, beavers have built a dam nearby and other changes have come, but this stream, this pool and this fish have come to symbolize all that is good about the trout streams of west central Alberta. This was my first sizable fish from this region, and its capture became a defining, watershed experience that drew me into a lifelong love affair with the small trout streams of the West Country.

The Big Picture

The Red Deer and North Saskatchewan rivers begin near each other in the Rockies of western Alberta and ultimately unite as major components of the Saskatchewan River, which flows into Hudson Bay. But like twins separated at birth, great distance is traveled and different paths are taken before the reunion. The North Saskatchewan flows northeastward through Rocky Mountain House and Edmonton before it swings east and leaves Alberta. The Red Deer River flows northeast to the city of Red Deer, then takes a hard right, gathering water from the northern half of the South Saskatchewan Basin.

To a scientist there are undoubtedly major differences between the Red Deer and North Saskatchewan systems. To a trout fisher, however, there are major similarities, which is why they will be examined together here. In both systems today, the dominant sport-fish are brown, cutthroat and bull trout.

The mainstem Red Deer and North Saskatchewan rivers and many of their tributaries begin in the Rockies of Banff and Jasper national parks as melting snow and ice. The headwater streams are cold, clean and low on the nutrients and algae crucial to aquatic life. With some exceptions, like the Cline River above Abraham Lake, most streams are not productive fisheries until they move out from the shadow of the Rockies and into the foothills.

In both systems the tributaries provide better fishing than the main stems of the big rivers. The reason is instability, but from two different sources. The upper Red Deer flows through a wide, braided gravel floodplain and undergoes a severe runoff each spring that not only scours the algae off the gravel but frequently changes the course of the river through its bed. The North Saskatchewan is controlled by the Bighorn Dam, a major power producer located east of Banff National Park. The discharge of water from the dam is very irregular, causing great fluctuation in water levels downstream. In both cases the instability is a detriment to trout production.

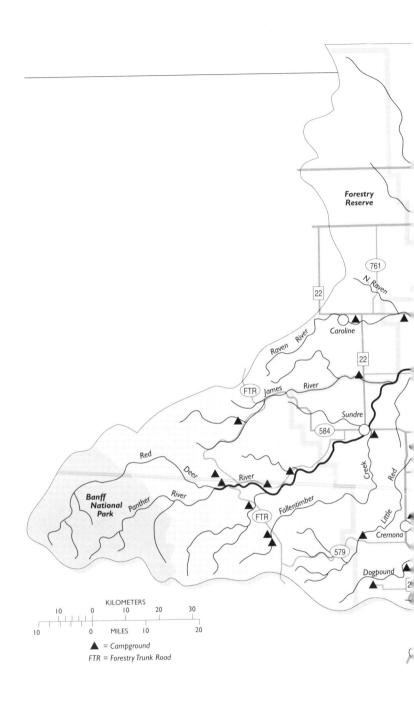

Red Deer River Basin

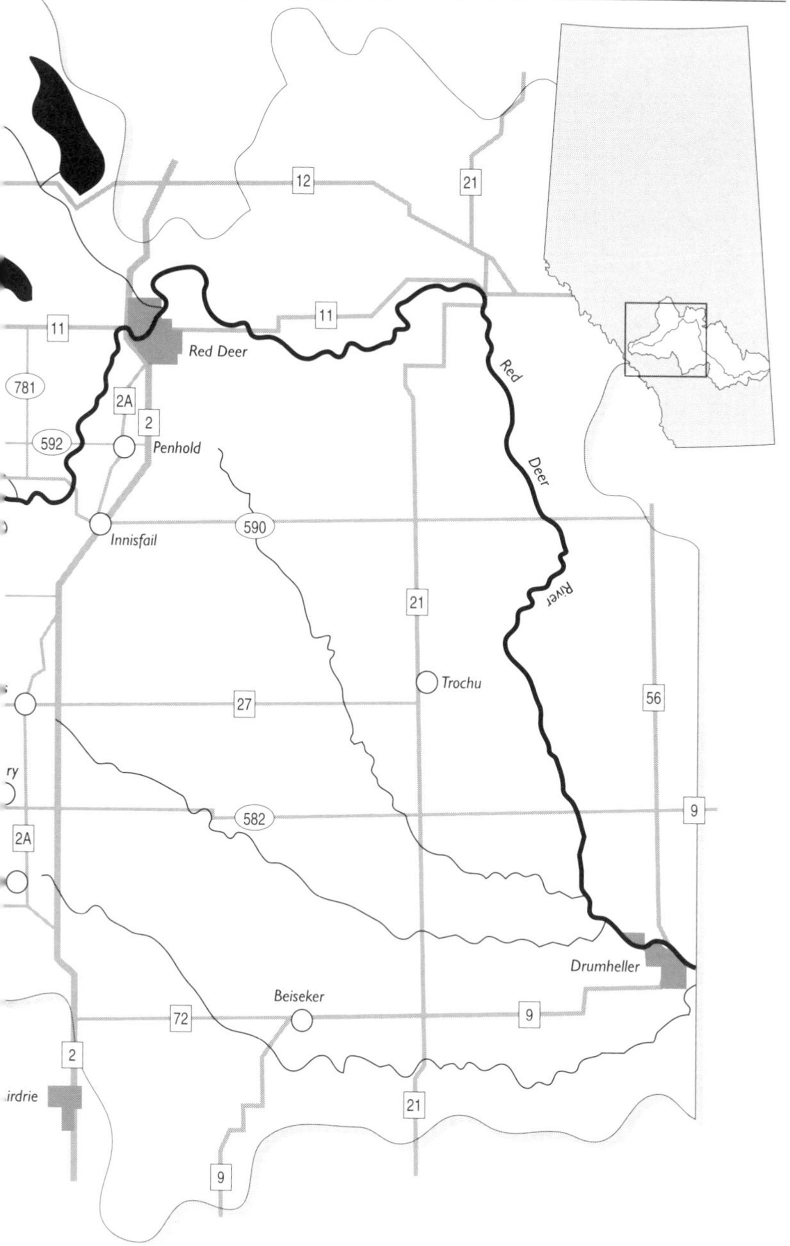

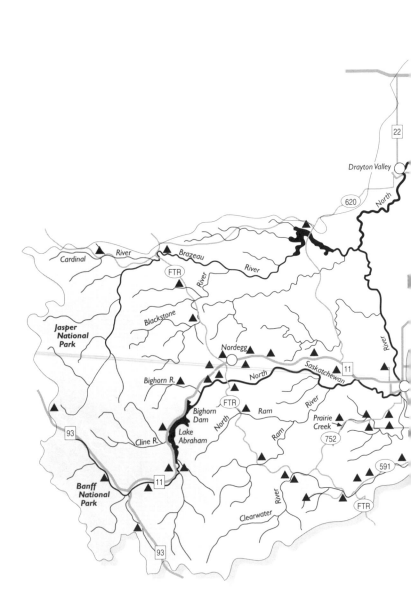

North Saskatchewan River Basin

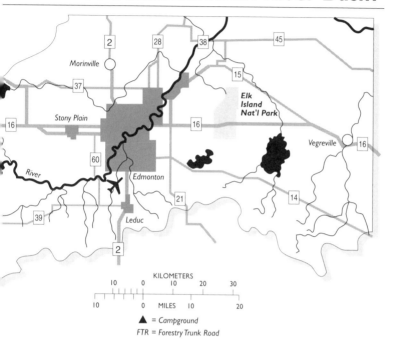

KILOMETERS

▲ = Campground

FTR = Forestry Trunk Road

Many of our best brown trout streams lie in an area roughly between the towns of Rocky Mountain House and Cochrane and extending from Highway 22 in the east to the Forestry Trunk Road in the west. Most of these foothill tributaries to the Red Deer and North Saskatchewan begin some distance east of the Rockies and consequently are less subject to the influence of mountain snowmelt than their headwater cousins. These streams have a short, local runoff early in the spring when the snow along the creeks melts, but they are usually in good fishing condition when the bigger rivers are still high and dirty from mountain runoff. This is gentle country where flat farmland gives way to easy foothills while evergreen forest mixes with aspen parkland, open meadows, cattle pastures and willow bogs.

This West Country is quietly haunted by Alberta's near-legendary fly-fishers: Barry Mitchell, Lloyd Shea, Don Andersen, Bob Scammell, Ray Cotton, Chris MacDonald, Don Cahoon, Bruce Goodall and others who creep around in secretive ways, fishing on weekdays and parking their trucks in thick stands of trees where you and I will never find them. These guys know their trout streams, and they flit like shadows from the North Raven to the Dogpound, leaving cold trails through cafe parking lots in Cremona, Water Valley, Caroline and Sundre.

There are a number of good streams in this area with similar characteristics, including the North and South Raven rivers, Prairie Creek, Fallen Timber Creek, the Little Red Deer River, Dogpound Creek, the James River, the Clearwater River, Shunda Creek, the Tay River, Clear Creek, Cow Creek and Alford Creek. These streams would all be classed as small to medium in size, and most flow through stream beds made at least partly of soil rather than gravel or rock. The earthen stream beds provide nutrients to the water, but they also allow the streams to dirty quickly after heavy rains. More positively, they also allow the development of a very important type of trout habitat—the undercut bank—which brown trout everywhere seem to love. And while there is plenty of variety here, the gentle slope of most streams produces a noticeable abundance of slow water.

While the waters here do grow good-sized trout—frequently in the sixteen- to twenty-inch range—most of them carry relatively low numbers of fish for reasons that are not entirely clear. There is no shortage of food, as many of these streams carry both abundant and diverse insect populations, so the problem may be a shortage of suitable spawning, rearing or wintering water.

One thing that is clear is that these streams have temperamental and fickle personalities. It is easy to have terrific fishing one day and not see a fish the next. They hold tight to their secrets and consistent success is a product of dedication and repetition. The people who spend a lot of time on these streams do quite well, but anglers who fish them only occasionally are often disappointed. However, under the right conditions, such as when a major hatch is in progress, the fishing can be exceptional.

Many of the best insect hatches occur on the Red Deer and North Saskatchewan tributaries in a relatively short period in late spring and early summer. Our largest common mayflies, the Western Green Drake and the Brown Drake, both hatch in June. The green, whose official name is *Ephemerella grandis,* lives in riffle areas with a gravel bottom and the Brown Drake, *Ephemera simulans,* is found in slow water with a soft, silty bottom. Green Drakes hatch each afternoon for a couple of weeks, and Brown Drakes emerge late in the evening or at night, but only for a few days. The Brown Drake is one of the highlights of the hatch calendar in the foothills brown trout streams, for it usually emerges heavily and often brings the biggest fish to the surface. It's also one of the easiest hatches to miss because it lasts such a short time. I've missed it many times and hit it perfectly just often enough to remember why I keep trying.

A much easier insect to find is the size 14 or 16 yellow-olive mayfly we call a Pale Morning Dun. Though it rarely hatches as heavily as the Brown Drake, it is usually around for about a month, beginning in early to mid-June in the West Country. It corresponds nicely to evening emergences of caddisflies, which the fish also like.

A number of these foothill streams have small sections of fast, rocky water, which is ideal habitat for the largest species of stoneflies. Both the giant black stonefly, called the Salmon-fly, and the golden stone hatch from these waters in June. Late summer is grasshopper time throughout the West, and many foothill streams provide good hopper fishing, which begins in late July or early August, particularly in areas around hayfields or open meadows. By late September many of these streams will be low and very clear, and the fish will be skittish and easily frightened. Longer, finer leaders and small terrestrial flies like red or black ants are good choices then. Cloudy, cool autumn days bring the universal Blue-winged Olive hatch and good fishing for rising trout. When a good hatch is in progress on one of these creeks and the fish are rising nicely, everything seems to be in order. You know where the fish are, you know they are feeding and all is well with the world.

Ah, but what if the fish aren't rising? That's when these streams even the score. It's also when an angler with experience on a particular stream has a huge advantage over an occasional visitor. Some of the good-looking water here doesn't hold many trout, and if the fish aren't showing themselves, a newcomer can fish over a lot of empty water without knowing it. When the trout aren't rising the experienced angler has the advantage of being able to concentrate on the places where he has found trout in the past, knowing that the slippery little critters are probably still there.

An angler new to the stream is wise to prospect with a dry fly or a streamer during nonhatch times. I like the dry fly to be an imitation of the largest insect the trout have been feeding on in the last couple of weeks. In late summer it will be a grasshopper, but earlier in the year it might be a Green Drake or Salmonfly imitation. I find it best to move quickly and concentrate on the best holding water.

A small streamer, like an olive or brown Woolly Bugger or a Spring Creek Bugger, can be a surprisingly effective weapon on these small brown trout streams at times. These flies can be fished on a floating line, and the best approach is to work the fly quickly through each pocket or run that might hold a fish. Sometimes the fish are willing to chase a streamer but reluctant to grab it. It can be frustrating to see fish swirling and boiling around your fly without actually eating it, but it is one way to take inventory quickly on an unfamiliar stream and begin building your list of known fish houses. Nymph-fishing can also be productive, especially in areas of fast, bouldery stonefly water and in the riffly water at the heads of deeper pools.

To me the greatest puzzle on these West Country waters is how to handle the many stretches of slow, deep water when the trout aren't rising. I've lain awake nights worrying about this and have tested numerous theories, none with enough success to be worth recounting here. I'll let you know when I have it figured out.

There are some streams in the North Saskatchewan and Red Deer systems with characteristics noticeably different from the foothill brown trout creeks. These streams rise farther west and are accessible from the Forestry Trunk Road. Notable here are the Panther River, the Ram and Clearwater systems and a number of north-bank tributaries to the North Saskatchewan, including the Bighorn and Cline rivers as well as the Cardinal and Blackstone, which empty into the Brazeau River.

These streams are closer to the mountains, and they look, feel and even smell different from the brown trout creeks just a few miles east. Though subject to mountain runoff and discoloration from heavy rain, the water in the high country streams gets very clear late in the summer and carries no hint of the tea-colored stain that is common in some of the brown trout creeks. The water flows over clean gravel and cobble, and pools follow riffles in a classic pattern. The water is cold and usually doesn't reach an ideal angling temperature until well into summer, making August and September the ideal months. This is wild country, and while you expect to see a moose or whitetail near the North Raven, it might be an elk or grizzly out here. Dense, dark evergreen timber flanks the rivers, and even in summer the pungent aroma of spruce carries a hint of melting snow from the big rocks farther west.

At this higher elevation the aquatic environment is harsh, and though you occasionally find brookies, browns or rainbows, the true stars of the high country are cutthroats and bull trout. Cutthroats are loved by fly-fishers for their great desire to feed on the surface—whether there's a hatch in progress or not. Traditional attractor patterns like Trudes, Humpys and Wulffs have probably fooled more cutthroats in Alberta than any other flies. So, while studious hatch-matching plays a relatively minor role in cutthroat fishing, there are some important insects that can make good fishing even better. There are golden stoneflies and Western Green Drake mayflies in the high country, and for reasons of water temperature and elevation, they hatch as much as a month later here than in the foothill brown trout streams.

The cutthroats sometimes forsake their preference for dry flies early in the season or when the water is heavily fished, such as the North Ram River can be on weekends in the summer. At these times they are often more receptive to a well-presented nymph like a Pennstone or a Bead Head Prince.

For many years bull trout have been a relatively small factor in the sport-fishing opportunities in this part of Alberta, owing to the well-documented decline in their numbers. Bull trout are a unique and appealing fish whose fundamental objective in life is to kill and eat things. Consequently bulls are best pursued with large streamer flies, which seem to satisfy their neurotic need for violence. I'm optimistic that the recently introduced no-kill regulation will allow these great beasts to recover and return to some of their former glory.

If you're doing it right this high country fishing will make it easy to sleep well at night because you'll be putting plenty of miles on the soles of your waders through the day. The fish are in the best pools, and the best pools are often some distance apart. The water will tantalize you and lead you on, the way trout streams always do, and it's easy to find yourself several miles from your vehicle before you decide to turn around and start back.

The most logical fly-fishing outfit for streams in the Red Deer and North Saskatchewan systems is a 4- or 5-weight floating line on a matching rod that is between eight and nine feet long. A sink-tip fly line can occasionally be useful for early season streamer-fishing.

New Fisheries

Good news for the future of Alberta's trout fishing is the rate at which "new" fisheries are developing. Some of these are indeed new fisheries—places with trout today that didn't have them yesterday. Others are reclamation projects—streams with severe problems that are being corrected in the hope of returning them to the realm of troutfulness.

Little practical fishing information is available for most of these places because the details are still being discovered and worked out by anglers. I expect it to be a great challenge and opportunity—mine and yours—to learn about these waters as they develop into productive fisheries in the coming years.

The first of these is the "new" Red Deer River below the Dickson Dam. The dam, built upstream of the town of Innisfail in the mid-1980s, was not without controversy locally, and like the Oldman Dam in southern Alberta, its construction was opposed by many Albertans for environmental and economic reasons.

The purpose of the dam and the reservoir, which is called Lake Gleniffer, is to allow Alberta to store water and deliver it to the province of Saskatchewan through the summer, thereby allowing more of the water in the Bow and Oldman systems to be retained for irrigation in the dry parts of southern Alberta. Like the Oldman Dam, this is a water-storage dam, so the volume of water released to the river is relatively stable, at about 2,200 cubic feet per second. And because the water is drawn from the bottom of the dam, it is cool and quite constant in temperature.

Cool water and stable flows are essential ingredients in a productive trout fishery. Another is a population of trout. Historically this portion of the Red Deer did not hold a lot of trout, so a supplementary source was needed to jump start the development of this fishery. In 1991 a thousand two-year-old brown trout from the Allison Creek Brood Trout Station were introduced to the Red Deer, but what was really needed was a strain of wild brown trout that lived in a river similar to the Red Deer. In the fall of 1992 biologists caught one thousand browns in the Bow River downstream of Calgary and transferred them to this section of the Red Deer River. Young fish were taken so they would be able to spawn several times in their new home.

As with the Oldman River, there are hopes that a productive tailwater fishery will develop in the Red Deer over the next few years. The jury is still out, but there are some encouraging signs. Fall studies have shown a steady increase in the number of spawning redds in this part of the Red Deer, from 43 in 1991 to 154 in 1994.

As of 1995, brown trout have occasionally been reported downstream as far as the city of Red Deer, but the number of catchable browns in this water is still relatively small. Currently the river fishes quite well in the fall, when the fish begin to concentrate below the dam prior to spawning. This is a river to watch, however, and everyone is hopeful that a new fishery—perhaps a new Bow River-caliber fishery—might develop near the city of Red Deer.

The most logical way to fish this water is to float it in a boat, but currently access is somewhat limited. There is a twelve- to fourteen-mile float from the dam to the Highway 54 bridge northwest of Innisfail, but because of slow water through the second half, it is a longer trip than most people like. Another option is a seven-mile float from Highway 54 to the bridge on Highway 592 near Penhold.

The river in this section is wadable but not crossable. It is in a stable, mostly unbraided channel, flowing through pretty country with high, steep banks reminiscent of the Bow downstream of Calgary.

The second cause for optimism about the future of Alberta's trout fishing is found in the successful restoration of the North Raven River, which has served as both inspiration and a model for work on a couple of other similar streams in the West Country. Clear Creek rises from a spring very near the source of the North Raven but flows in the opposite direction, northwest into the Clearwater River. The creek has long carried a population of brown and brook trout, but like the North Raven of the 1960s, it was damaged by cattle and beavers to the extent that it became little more than a connected series of wide, muddy ponds. The stream essentially had to be rebuilt.

A restoration project was initiated in 1991 by Trout Unlimited Canada and funded by the Environmental Partners Fund, Alberta Fish and Wildlife, Alberta Transportation and Shell Oil. Stream banks were fenced, beaver dams were removed and deflectors were installed to deepen and narrow the creek channel. With time it is hoped Clear Creek will provide fishing of a quality equal to that of its more famous cousin.

Dogpound Creek is not, strictly speaking, a spring creek though it has some definite spring creek characteristics. It is a small gentle stream that drains out of the Stoney Indian Reserve northwest of Cochrane and flows considerable distance to its confluence with the Little Red Deer River, east of Sundre.

Dogpound also has been damaged by cattle and beavers over the years though not to the degree that Clear Creek has. The work on Dogpound began in 1985 and has included the removal of beaver dams, the construction of fences to restrict cattle to certain sections of the stream and the installation of deflectors, log walls and other habitat-improving devices. This work has been undertaken by Alberta Fish and Wildlife with cooperation and crucial assistance from local landowners, Trout Unlimited and the Petro Canada Flyfishing Club in Calgary.

The third source of faith in the future is the development of the North Ram River's catch-and-release cutthroat fishery, which has inspired the Alberta government in an attempt to duplicate the feat by introducing west-slope cutthroats to a number of other North Saskatchewan tributaries. The Bighorn River joins the North Saskatchewan a short distance below Abraham Lake, and cutthroats were introduced to the river above Crescent Falls in the early 1990s. Similar plantings have been made in the Cardinal and Blackstone rivers, which flow into the Brazeau River, and Wapiabi Creek, which is a tributary of the Blackstone. Some of these waters had native bull trout in them originally while others had no fish at all, as was the case in the North Ram. Cutthroats from elsewhere in the system have found their way into the Cline River, which flows into Abraham Lake, and a good fishery is developing there as well.

The waters of the North Saskatchewan and Red Deer rivers drain an immense area of Alberta and offer a tremendous variety of fly-fishing opportunity. The veteran fly-fisher seeking a challenge will find all of it he can stand in the brown trout streams of the Caroline–Rocky Mountain House region. The new fly-fisher or youngster will find perfect "learner streams" like Shunda or Elk creeks, where the trout are small but eager. The angler seeking beauty and solitude will be drawn to the high country for cutthroats and the possibility of giant bull trout. Few anglers will find enough time to explore all the potential offered by these two river systems.

THE GREAT WATERS: *The North Raven River (also called Stauffer Creek)*

There is no fence-sitting when it comes to this stream, which is a Red Deer River tributary located north and east of the town of Caroline. People love it or despise it. Some I've sent to fish it for the first time have returned glassy-eyed and in love. Others have returned and called me in the middle of the night to ask, "What did I do to deserve that?"

In the list of things to love are some undeniable facts. It is a spring creek—the best of a very few in Alberta—and consequently it is very stable, neither running off in spring nor dirtying up with summer rains. It is easily accessible. It has good insect hatches. It grows big fish.

What could possibly be wrong with all this? Listen. The stream is slow, clear, deep, narrow and almost completely lined with thick willows. The bottom is silty and hard to wade in. The fish are moody and paranoid, and most fly-fishers don't even see let alone catch the big browns the biologists tell us are so abundant.

So, though the creek looks innocent enough when you glance at it from your car at the bridge south of the Stauffer Store, don't be fooled. Beneath that bright, bubbly smile lurks a cruel, unforgiving heart. One moment it is all grace and beauty, the very essence of what a trout stream should be. Around the next bend it is hell with mayflies, a place that seems to have been designed for revenge. Yet, for all its fickle nature, the North Raven is a stream I can't get enough of.

The creek slides clear and cold out of springs on the Leavitt and Hankinson farms north of Caroline, and gently rolls about fifteen miles south and east to its confluence with the South Raven River near Highway 54. Its spring-fed water is rich in minerals, including calcium, which stimulate the growth of aquatic plants. The weeds provide habitat for mayflies, caddisflies, backswimmers and midges. The upper portion of the stream is primarily brook trout water, but as it gathers additional spring flows, it becomes perfect brown trout habitat.

According to the late Dr. Bill Parsons, brown trout made their appearance in the North Raven in 1930 courtesy of a government game manager whose name seems to have been lost over the years. He was obviously an astute, dedicated angler, though, for he recognized the stream's potential and noted its similarity to the chalk streams of his native England. Without a word to the authorities or anyone else, he dumped a few hundred brown trout into the creek.

The fish thrived and gradually the North Raven became known to a few local anglers. The quality of its fishing and its reputation increased for a time, but eventually the creek fell on hard times at the hands of the common culprit called Progress. Road construction and oil exploration caused problems, and grazing cattle did severe damage to the stream bed. Over time the creek's stable, grassy banks became wide expanses of muddy, sticky goo. The stream became wider and shallower, and the critical spawning gravel was gradually covered by silt.

In 1974, through the cooperation of the Alberta Fish and Game Association and the provincial Buck For Wildlife Program, a restoration effort was begun. Fences were built to restrict the cattle's access to the water, and rock structures were installed to narrow the stream bed and increase current velocity to gradually remove the silt. The program has been a great success, and old-timers say the creek now looks much like it did in the good old days. Today the major problem faced by the creek is an overabundance of beavers, which like to turn moving water into still water. Work continues on the

North Raven in the 1990s, largely at the urging of the creek's staunchest protectors, Barry Mitchell of Red Deer and Don Andersen of Rocky Mountain House.

The most popular section of the North Raven is between the bridge on Secondary Highway 761 and the next road west, and there are convenient parking areas at both spots. Though these bridges are only two miles apart, the creek meanders and doubles back such that there are probably six miles of water between them. The stream here is fifteen to thirty feet wide and moves gently under a glassy surface. It supports about thirteen hundred brown trout per mile, a statistic many anglers find hard to believe.

Over time the little creek has chewed away at its earthen edges, creating deep holes and undercut banks at every bend. Deadfall and debris clutter the holes, and willows line most of the banks. There is very little broken water. A fly-fisher must usually get into the creek to find back-cast room, and must cast and progress upstream to stay out of the fish's sight and avoid spooking them. If ever there was a creek that needed a 1- or 2-weight fly line, this is it. Here the fishing is difficult yet possible, but in the lower reaches of the creek it is nearly impossible because the water is too deep to wade and the banks too brushy to penetrate.

Though the spring at the stream's source keeps the upper portion of the North Raven free of ice the entire year, it is a cold spring (about 40° F) and the creek does not fish particularly well in winter. The fishing gets interesting in May, when the trout become active and begin to feed more frequently. And a little later yet, when the snipe whistle and the wolf-willows bloom, this becomes a stream to yearn for. June is show time in this part of Alberta, and the North Raven is one of the stars. Pale Morning Duns, caddis, and Brown and Green Drakes all hatch then, and even the big fish are drawn out from under the banks to feed on the surface.

If an angler is very good and very lucky, he might actually hook one of the big fish, but the heavy weed growth and thick brush along the banks put his chances of landing one somewhere between slim and fat. There are five-pound browns in this stream, but even veteran North Raven anglers are pleased to land the occasional trout half that size.

Brown Drake

Through the first half of the summer it is wise to fish the popular section of the North Raven through the week rather than on weekends. May and June bring out plenty of anglers, and it is easy for them to get in each other's way. The stream is small enough that the fish are disturbed each time someone wades up the creek, and an angler who is a half hour behind another will wonder where all the fish have gone.

From July to the end of October the creek receives much less fishing pressure, in part because of the difficulty posed by the heavy weed growth. Through the summer there are frequent hatches of smaller mayflies and caddisflies, and there is a particularly good late-season emergence of Blue-winged Olive mayflies. Backswimmers and hoppers are also active in August and September.

A juicy bend on the North Raven River.

A fly-fisher usually finishes a day on the North Raven tired, bruised and sweaty—physically worn out from tramping through the willow morass and emotionally drained by the intense nature of the fishing. He rarely returns feeling smug; *humble* is usually a better word.

A friend of mine recently decided that the best way to learn something about this stream would be to fish it exclusively for a whole summer. He did that, and when I talked to him in September he said the questions still outnumbered the answers by about three to one.

If the North Raven were a person it would be a beautiful, petite woman who had a black belt in karate, the kind of lady who could break both your legs and never stop smiling. This is not a stream for beginners. In time though, there are many lessons to be learned from this fickle temptress, and once you have paid your dues here, you can be comfortable on any small stream in the world.

There are some of us—and I'm only a little embarrassed to admit being one—who take a perverse delight in occasionally being mugged and humiliated by a trout stream. And there is no stream more capable of it than this innocent little gem that gurgles through the swamp northeast of Caroline.

Access and Accommodation

Many of the foothill brown trout streams in this part of west central Alberta are easily accessible from Highway 22 and a system of secondary gravel roads that are shown in good detail on *The Fishin' Map.* Motel accommodation is available in Sundre, Caroline, Cremona and Rocky Mountain House. Most of the best streams boast at least one provincial campground.

The Forestry Trunk Road (Highway 40) crosses both the North and South Ram rivers and provides access to the Clearwater, James and upper Red Deer rivers and tributaries. There also are numerous campgrounds on the trunk road. Highway 11 provides access to the Cline and Bighorn river areas. Motels are somewhat scarce in the high country, and the most convenient ones are in Rocky Mountain House, Nordegg, Sundre, at the Cline River Crossing on Highway 11 at Abraham Lake, and at the intersection of Highways 11 and 93 in Banff National Park at Saskatchewan River Crossing.

Good foot access to the Red Deer River below the Dickson Dam can be gained from the dam itself or from secondary roads leading south from Highway 54.

Hatch Chart for Foothills Streams

Date	Hatch	Imitation
April 15 – May 15	Blue-winged Olive	Adams, Crystal Blue-winged Olive, size 18, 20
May 1 – June 1	March Brown	Adams, Quad March Brown, size 14
May 15 – Aug 30	Caddis	Elk Hair Caddis, size 12 – 18
May 25 – June 15	Salmonfly	Orange Stimulator, size 4 – 8

June 10 – July 5	Brown Drake	Brown Paradrake, Crystal Brown Drake, size 8, 10
June 10 – July 1	Western Green Drake	Olive Paradrake, Crystal Green Drake, size 10
June 15 – July 20	Pale Morning Dun	Pale Morning Dun Parachute, size 16
July 20 – Sept 15	Grasshopper	Dave's Hopper, Hopper-cator, size 6 – 12
Sept 1 – Oct 15	Blue-winged Olive	Adams, Crystal Blue-winged Olive, size 18, 20

Hatch Chart for High Country Streams

Date	*Hatch*	*Imitation*
June 1 – Aug 30	Caddis	Elk Hair Caddis, size 12 – 18
July 1 – Aug 15	Golden Stonefly	Yellow Stimulator, size 6 – 10

July 10 – Aug 15	Western Green Drake	Olive Paradrake, Crystal Green Drake, size 10
Aug 10 – Sept 15	Grasshopper	Dave's Hopper, Hopper-cator, size 6 – 12
Aug 15 – Sept 15	Blue-winged Olive	Adams, Crystal Blue-winged Olive, size 18, 20

9

The ATHABASCA
RIVER SYSTEM

I N OCTOBER 1995 an angler went fishing for burbot in the
Athabasca River near Hinton. Instead of a burbot he
caught an enormous bull trout. We'll never know exactly
how big this fish was, for it was dutifully released as the regulations require. The fish was somewhere between thirty-nine
and forty-three inches long, with a twenty-three-inch girth.
The angler estimated it at twenty-five pounds, but Kerry
Brewin, chairman of the Bull Trout Task Force, calculated its
weight at thirty-four pounds. This fish was obviously the
Chairman of the Board. It was at worst an Alberta record bull
and at best a world record. It seems fitting that such a fish
was caught the same year the bull trout was named Alberta's
provincial fish and given the protection it so desperately
needs.

The biggest trout I've caught in the Athabasca system
could have been eaten in one gulp by this monster, but I did
catch some memorable trout when I was learning to fly-fish in
the late 1960s. July 20, 1969, the day Neil Armstrong hopped
out of the Lunar Excursion Module and made man's most historic footprints, I was not in front of the TV but fishing a
beaver pond on a small tributary to the Athabasca River. The

pond has since silted in as they eventually do, but in those days I fished it three or four times every year. Just about the time Armstrong was making his short, famous speech from the surface of the moon, I saw a big fish cruise along the shadow of a fallen tree. I had never seen a fish more than eight inches long in this pond, but this one looked at least twice that size.

I'm sure the suspense has leaked out of this story by now, so I'll save paper and say, yes, I did catch the fish and, yes, it was sixteen inches long. Later, as I lay in the sleeping bag inside the tent, I felt particularly pleased, as if I had cleared a hurdle and accomplished something. I often struggled with fly-fishing in those days and sometimes wondered if I should keep doing it. This fish helped build my confidence and seal my fate. It was an historic day—both for mankind and a teenaged fly-fisher. One small step for Jim.

THE BIG PICTURE

The Athabasca River begins in a tongue of the Columbia Icefield in Jasper National Park. It is big, fast and glacial white. From its confluence with the Sunwapta River it flows north through peaks and glaciers worthy of the best beer commercials and lays a path for part of the Banff–Jasper Highway, regarded as one of the most spectacular mountain roads in the world. But for all its grandeur, the upper Athabasca is an alpine river lacking the nutrients essential to sustaining large populations of fish. In Jasper National Park many of its gravelly, wide-open tributaries, like the Snaring, Rocky and Fiddle rivers, have small populations of small rainbows and brook trout along with whitefish and bull trout. The Miette River, west of the town of Jasper, is a slower, deeper stream carrying the same mix of fish. In the less accessible northern part of the park is the Snake Indian River, which has good fishing for bull trout, and its tributary, Blue Creek, also is very good for bulls and rainbows. The best streams in Jasper National Park are the ones draining out of lakes, for they are usually clear and more productive than the glacier-fed streams.

As the Athabasca leaves the shining mountains behind and heads northeast from Hinton, it gathers tributaries from the Willmore Wilderness, north of Jasper Park. Once out of the shadow of the Rockies the landscape is dominated by rolling hills of lodgepole pine and lowlands of muskeg and willow.

The Athabasca River flows into Lake Athabasca in the northeastern corner of Alberta and then on to the Arctic Ocean as part of first the Slave and then the Mackenzie rivers. There are more than twelve hundred miles of cold-water streams in the Athabasca drainage carrying native rainbows, bull trout, mountain whitefish and arctic grayling, as well as some introduced brook and brown trout. Trout and whitefish are most abundant upstream of the confluence of the Athabasca and McLeod rivers at Whitecourt while grayling are common in Athabasca tributaries from Hinton all the way to Lake Athabasca.

Athabasca Tributaries

Outside of Jasper National Park the Athabasca River is big and silty through much of the season, and fly-fishers are more often attracted to its tributaries. These include the Berland and McLeod river systems, the upper Pembina and, farther downstream, the smaller Freeman River on the southeast slopes of the Swan Hills.

The best streams in the Berland system are the mainstem Berland itself, the Little Berland and Wildhay rivers, all of which carry arctic grayling, mountain whitefish, rainbows and bull trout, and all of which are accessible from Highway 40 north of Hinton.

The McLeod River begins in the mountains south of Hinton near the village of Cadomin and flows north and east toward Edson before swinging north again to join the Athabasca at the town of Whitecourt. This river and its tributaries have been popular with anglers since the coal mining industry began to thrive in the early 1900s. The Hinton–Robb area has long been known locally as the Coal Branch. Small native Athabasca rainbows, bull trout and whitefish live in the upper McLeod, and grayling become common near Edson. North of Highway 16 the best McLeod tributaries are the Edson River, Sundance, Little Sundance and Trout creeks, and south of the highway, the Embarrass and Gregg rivers.

Today the best fishing in the Athabasca drainage outside Jasper National Park is in the least accessible areas though finding such areas requires exploration and research. The main rivers provide very good fly-fishing for mountain whitefish in the fall, though few anglers consider these fish a worthy target.

The larger rivers in the system are primarily freestone in nature with gravel and cobble bottoms. Many of the smaller streams, though, flow through willow or muskeg bogs and often have numerous beaver dams on them. Their water frequently carries a slight tea-colored stain from tannin in the muskeg. The bogs and beaver dams also keep these streams relatively stable and allow them to remain clear after heavy rains.

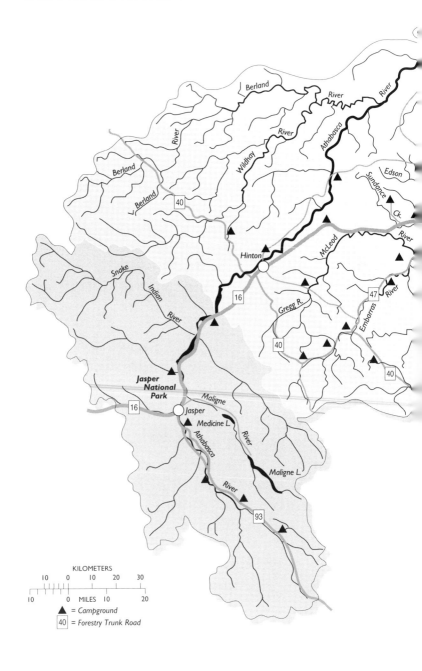

KILOMETERS

10   0   10   20   30

10   0   MILES   10   20

▲ = Campground

[40] = Forestry Trunk Road

Athabasca River Basin

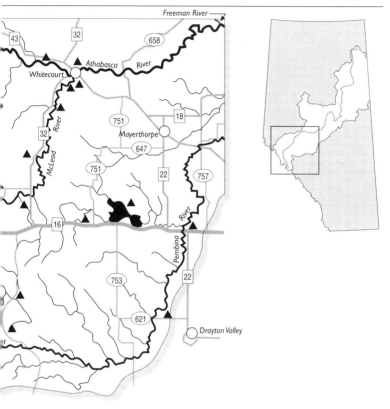

Beaver activity on a trout stream can be a two-edged sword. While beaver dams can silt up the stream bottom and block trout's migration to spawning water, they also provide places for fish to live and overwinter. There are hundreds of good beaver ponds in the Athabasca system, many with rainbow trout in them. Some of the best are on Sundance Creek, the Edson River and Drinnan Creek south of Hinton. Many of these smaller streams are overgrown to the point of being difficult to fish. While the Athabasca itself is best fished with a 6- or 7-weight fly rod, the smaller tributaries usually require something in the 3- to 5-weight range. Some tiny creek specialists prefer very short six- to seven-foot fly rods, which allow them to keep their casts under the overhanging tree limbs and brush.

Nymphs like Pheasant Tails, Zug Bugs and Hare's Ears work well in early season, but by late June there are decent hatches of mayflies and caddis. The trout here are more opportunistic than selective, and it is unusual for a well-presented Adams, Elk Hair Caddis or Humpy to be refused by a fish that is already looking up.

The occasional exception to this is when our friend the mountain whitefish gets serious about feeding on the surface. When this happens he is usually eating tiny flies—often midges—and though we snooty fly-fishers would never admit it, rising whitefish are often harder to catch than trout.

The stream fishing season outside Jasper Park is short. The major rivers are open from April 1 to October 31, but runoff keeps them dirty for a couple of weeks between mid-May and late June. Most of the tributaries are open only between June 16 and August 31.

Trouble in the Watershed

I have fond memories of these streams in the upper Athabasca system, but it has been many years since I have visited them, and in researching their status today, I am disturbed by what I find. Much of the good news I have related about Alberta's trout rivers unfortunately does not apply to the Athabasca system. The problem appears to be a case of the right fish living in the wrong circumstances. This area has a short growing season, and the native fish all mature very slowly and must spend as much as six to eight years in the stream before they can spawn. Grayling and bull trout are both very easy to catch, and one of the traditions in this part of the world is the desire for a heavy creel. Catch-and-release fishing has never become fashionable here, and most of the fish caught are taken home.

Though this is a rugged part of Alberta, a good map reveals a countryside sliced into small pieces by hundreds of roads, trails and cutlines developed for the oil and timber industries. These trails and the growing popularity of all-terrain vehicles, quads, trail bikes and mountain bikes has allowed deep human penetration into formerly inaccessible areas. And given the relative proximity to the major city of Edmonton, there are plenty of people available to do the penetrating.

When the land is accessible and the fish are easily caught and killed before they are old enough to spawn, the result is overharvest and a declining population of fish. The problem is not new, for complaints of deteriorating fishing in the McLeod River began at least as far back as the 1940s. Today the complaints often sound like this: "I used to take a limit of fish from that stream ten or twelve times a season, and now I can hardly find a fish. Somebody should do something." Welcome to the frontier.

Except for an occasional big bull trout, you'll not find

many large fish in these streams either. This is partly a natural characteristic of the watershed, but it has been accentuated by decades of overharvest.

Logging has been another source of difficulty for the trout of the Athabasca system. Not only do logging roads open up the backcountry to people who want to take the fish home, but after the trees are taken there is nothing to hold the soil together, and the streams silt up quickly whenever there is a heavy rain. The silt gradually covers the gravel that the fish need for spawning.

Carl Hunt, biologist with the Fish and Wildlife Division's Edson office, believes there is now likely no harvestable surplus of fish in the streams in this area. He favors drastic reductions on creel limits for trout and whitefish, and complete no-kill regulations on arctic grayling. Unfortunately biologists working in the Athabasca system are in the difficult position of having little hard data with which to defend their positions. Severe population declines are very apparent but can't actually be proved because there are no previous figures to compare with today's population data.

A look at history is not comforting. In the past it has usually taken government a very long time to put restrictive regulations in place, even when their need was apparent. Biologists were calling for catch-and-release regulations on bull trout for fifteen years before it happened.

The fishing in the Athabasca system can be recovered, at least to a degree, if changes in management and anglers' attitudes occur quickly. But if it takes fifteen years it will probably be too late for the native rainbows and grayling of the Athabasca watershed.

I've often thought God must have smiled when He came up with the arctic grayling, for this is a beautiful fish that swims in beautiful places. It loves dry flies and is the perfect fish for young or new fly-fishers to chase. Years ago I caught a large grayling from a stream made accessible by a logging road. It was a spectacular male fish with a huge purple dorsal, black spots and striped pectoral fins. I killed him and was startled to see his dramatic colors fade and disappear almost immediately. Was he a metaphor for his species? Is somebody trying to tell us something? Are we listening?

THE GREAT WATERS: *The Maligne River*

The best of the streams draining lakes in Jasper National Park is the Maligne River below Maligne Lake. From a bridge at the outlet you can still look down into the water to check for trout, as I did each time I fished the river as a teenager. I once spotted a big brook trout that way and then tied a gaudy streamer in the cab of the truck before getting into the river and catching him. Though it was only a seventeen-year-old kid and a seventeen-inch brook trout, it was as close as I've ever come to the mythical notion of the observant angler creating a perfect fly at streamside before conquering the leviathan monster.

A short distance below the lake the river's slope increases and it becomes a fast, rocky white-water stream. Maligne means "wicked" or "evil" in French, and this water lives up to its name—so much so that portions of the 1954 movie *River of No Return* were filmed here. This water is too deep and too fast to be waded to any degree, so most of the fishing is done near the banks. There are plenty of eight- to fourteen-inch rainbows and brook trout in the small pockets amidst the froth and boulders, but occasionally you'll be surprised by a larger fish. It's hard to fish deep in this water, so I've come to prefer either dry flies, like Wulffs and Humpys, or streamers fished just under the surface.

The ferocious Maligne River downstream of Maligne Lake.

After nine miles of bobbing, weaving and dancing through the boulders, the swift Maligne enters the geological anomaly known as Medicine Lake. Paradoxically, though the sizable Maligne River flows into the south end of the lake, there is no outlet. Yet every autumn the water level in the lake recedes till nothing but the river channel remains. This was a great puzzle to the Indians and early visitors to Jasper National Park, but we now know the water drains into a system of underground channels through sink holes in the bottom of the lake. This creates a sizable underground river, carrying an estimated fourteen hundred cubic feet of water per second. Most of it reappears several miles downstream in Maligne Canyon and in some of the lakes near the Jasper Park Lodge. In the early days a concerned park warden tried to "correct" this problem in Medicine Lake by dumping old mattresses, magazines and debris into the sinkholes to try to plug the lake as if it were a bathtub.

By mid-September the lake is a wide mud flat with a slow blue river flowing through it. The trout are concentrated in the channel and the fishing is very good. Schools of rainbows cruise this water and anglers cast Hare's Ears to sighted fish or big dries to fish feeding on Grey Drake mayflies. The channel is too deep to be waded across, but it can be fished on foot though the mud is soft and the walking somewhat difficult.

Many of the fish are between one and two pounds, but some are larger. They are strong fish that perform well when hooked, often racing through the shallow mud flats like bonefish. Medicine Lake is regulated as "fly-fishing only" water for the entire open season, which extends from July 1 to October 31. The Maligne River is also reserved for fly-fishing only for the months of August and September. The upper Maligne system is easily accessible via a major paved road from the Jasper townsite.

ACCESS AND ACCOMMODATION

Most of the streams in the Hinton–Edson region are accessible from Highways 16, 40 and 47, and numerous secondary roads. Many of the best streams have campgrounds on them. The grayling streams between Whitecourt and Swan Hills are accessible from Highways 32 and 33, and secondary roads. Motel accommodation is available in Hinton, Edson and Whitecourt.

In Jasper National Park many streams are accessible from main roads. There are some exceptions, notably the Snake Indian and upper Astoria rivers. Campground and motel accommodation is available in and around the town of Jasper, but as in most popular national parks, reservations are sometimes needed to secure a space, particularly on weekends.

HATCH CHART

Date	Hatch	Imitation
April 20 – May 20	March Brown	Adams, Quad March Brown, size 14
April 20 – June 10	Blue-winged Olive	Adams, Crystal Blue-winged Olive, size 18, 20
April 20 – Sept 30	Caddis	Elk Hair Caddis, size 12 – 18

June 15 – July 15	Western Green Drake	Olive Paradrake, Crystal Green Drake, size 10
July 5 – Aug 10	Pale Morning Dun	Pale Morning Dun Parachute, size 16
Aug 1 – Sept 30	*Tricorythodes*	Trico Spinner, size 18, 20

10

The PEACE RIVER SYSTEM

I T'S SOMETIMES CALLED the Mighty Peace, and though that sounds pretty corny, my limited experience on it would cause me to concur. I fished the mainstem Peace once with Keith Roscoe, who was pretty sure the fishing would be better on the far side of the river. We paddled his canoe all the way across the huge river under warm, sunny skies. The fishing *was* pretty decent on the far side, but when we paddled back, dense, black thunderheads were being chased across the valley by a vicious wind. It was the only time I've seen whitecaps on a river. Though we made it back without incident, I paddled hard, driven by the same fear I'd have if I stalled my truck in the path of an oncoming train.

The Peace River Country has long been a destination for sport hunters pursuing moose, bears and geese, but it has never received much attention from fly-fishers. You don't read about it in the glossy fly-fishing magazines, and you don't see fishing videos filmed on its streams. Yet I have a friend who calls it the new frontier of western fly-fishing and another who considers it the last stronghold in the world for big bull trout. Do these guys draw a cheque from the Peace Country Tourism Department, or is there something going on here?

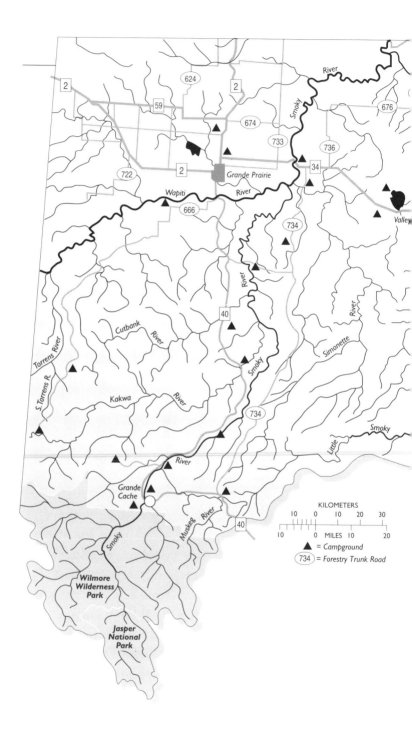

KILOMETERS

10   0   10   20   30

10   0   MILES 10   20

▲ = Campground

734 = Forestry Trunk Road

Peace River Basin

High Prairie

49

2

47

Fox Creek

The Big Picture

About thirty percent of Alberta's water is collected in the Peace River Basin, and of this, more than twelve hundred miles of rivers and streams carry bull trout, arctic grayling and mountain whitefish.

The Peace is the largest river to flow from British Columbia into Alberta. Its headwaters are in north central British Columbia, just across the Continental Divide from the beginnings of the Skeena system, whose tributaries form Canada's best-known wild steelhead fishery. By the time the Peace enters Alberta it is a huge river carrying twenty times the volume of the Bow. Though there is some good fly-fishing in the Peace itself in British Columbia, in Alberta it is a smooth-flowing, silty river known more for a high concentration of black bears in the river breaks than for its fishing potential.

White settlers were first drawn to the Peace Country two hundred years ago by the fur trade and more recently by agriculture. Today it is the most northerly grain-producing region on the continent, and over half of the lower Peace Basin is under cultivation. The farming boom is not over yet either, for this is one of the last places in Alberta where crown land is still being sold for agriculture.

This land continues to be greatly desired by people, and in the upper Peace Basin today the timber industry wants what grows up from the ground and the oil industry covets what flows beneath it.

Though there are cold-water fisheries throughout the Alberta portion of the Peace Basin, fly-fishers concentrate on a rough rectangle of land extending from Grande Cache and Grande Prairie west to the British Columbia border and east to the towns of Fox Creek and Valleyview. This is a big chunk of real estate—close to ten thousand square miles—but it represents a rather small portion of the basin. The streams of greatest interest to fly-fishers are Peace tributaries: the Smoky, Little Smoky, Kakwa, Simonette, Cutbank, Wapiti and Muskeg rivers.

These streams flow through valleys cut into foothills and low mountains flanked with lodgepole pine and white and black spruce. The country is rough, and the lowlands are thick with willow, alder and muskeg. It is classic boreal forest where predators and prey of all sizes are still abundant. Many streams begin in the muskeg of the foothills and are consequently free from the severe scouring of heavy spring runoff.

Grayling and bull trout are the featured performers here, and the fishing for both is exceptional. The arctic grayling is not known for its size (the world record is about six pounds) but rather for its beauty and its willingness to take dry flies. The streams of the Peace Country have grayling fishing equal to that in the more famous waters north of the 60th parallel, and many streams carry grayling that would surpass the current Alberta record.

Bull trout and arctic grayling form a fine complement to each other. A day well spent here would begin by fishing upstream, catching grayling on dry flies like the Adams and Black Gnat, and then after lunch turning around and working back down, scouring the pools with a size 4 Clouser Minnow for big bulls.

The best bull trout fishing in this area, and likely in just about any area, is in the Kakwa River, which is a tributary to the Smoky between Grande Cache and Grande Prairie. This large river has seen relatively few anglers over the years and is still full of bull trout that regularly reach five or six pounds and sometimes more.

Bull trout are known as meat-eaters, and given a small fish as a choice on the menu, they will take it every time. But some of the streams in the Peace system, notably the Little Smoky and Muskeg rivers, are rich in aquatic insects, and you also can catch bulls on nymphs like Bead Head Princes and Golden stoneflies.

Other than a few isolated and ill-advised plantings of brook trout, there have been few stockings of exotic species of fish to disturb the natural mix of natives in the Peace system. The only notable exception is the introduction of cutthroats into a formerly fishless reach of the Torrens River southwest of Grande Prairie. This one is turning out well, however, for these fish are now spawning successfully and occasionally reaching sixteen inches in length.

So why is the fishing so much better in the Peace system than the Athabasca? The answer lies partly in the inherent character of the Peace watershed. Here there are more rivers, bigger rivers, and many of them are free from the effects of spring flooding. Many streams maintain a higher mean summer temperature than streams with glacial sources and also have more consistent flows, particularly in winter. But the fishing is also better here because of circumstances that have kept the anglers from getting at the fish.

Though sizable portions of wilderness in the Peace drainage have been opened up by the oil, gas and timber industries, in many areas this process is still just beginning. The streams in the Peace drainage have simply not been accessible to anglers for as long as those in the Athabasca drainage. The Peace is also a larger system without a major city nearby, and angling pressure has therefore been lighter and more dispersed.

Most anglers prefer the second half of the summer on these streams, for it is then that water temperatures are at their peak and access to the streams is most reliable. A fairly light fly outfit can be used on most of the Peace system though anything lighter than a 4-weight might get you into trouble with a big Wapiti River bull trout. Though many of the rivers are big enough, float trips are difficult because of the lack of adequate boat access. Jet boats are sometimes used on the larger rivers by local anglers.

As always, the angling regulations should be consulted to determine the current status of bait bans, seasons and creel limits. Because of dioxins and furins in the sediment of the streams, the provincial government recommends that white-fish from these waters not be eaten.

THE GREAT WATERS: *The Little Smoky River*

In researching this book it has been comforting to see that every important stream has one or more guardian anglers who take it upon themselves to stand up and fight for the preservation of the fishery. Though I expected to find this on high-profile waters like the Bow and the Oldman, it was particularly encouraging to meet Darryl Smith, the unofficial keeper of the Little Smoky.

Darryl grew up fishing the streams of the Edson and Whitecourt area and first saw the waters of the Peace Country in 1979, when he moved to Valleyview to begin a dentistry career. Being single and a confirmed fly-fisher, he began to explore the streams in his new neighborhood and found him-self drawn to the wilderness portions of the Muskeg, Wapiti and Kakwa rivers. Then someone suggested he have a look at the Little Smoky. He hiked into a remote part of the river in 1980 and has never been the same since.

The upper Little Smoky is unlike any other stream in the Peace system and indeed unlike any other stream in Alberta. Through its upper sixty miles, water seeps up through springs in dense muskeg bog to feed the river. The water is crystal clear but with the slight tea-colored stain common to streams here. Aquatic vegetation grows heavily in this nutrient-rich water, and moss, pondweed and northern water milfoil cover a gravel and cobble bottom and provide habitat for dense populations of aquatic insects.

This river looks like, and essentially is, a spring creek. And like the famous spring creeks in Montana and Idaho, this one comes complete with rise forms on the surface and long shadows cruising the pools. But this is not Montana and these are not rainbows and browns. Instead, on this northern boreal spring creek, the risers are arctic grayling and the shadows are bull trout.

With his first visit Darryl Smith became obsessed with the Little Smoky River. He began to explore much of its considerable length, fishing its heavy hatches of mayflies and caddis. He began to keep records of the fishing, and for over ten years his catch rate has been in the range of nine to ten grayling per *hour*. He also began to fish streamers for the bull trout and found that four- to six-pounders were common and that every once in a while he could catch one near ten pounds.

Then he began to worry about his river. The fishing was holding up, but the countryside was being opened and developed at a ferocious rate, and he didn't wish to witness again what he had seen in the Athabasca system. In 1986 he introduced provincial biologists to the river and convinced them to begin gathering data on the fishery.

In 1988 he and other concerned anglers in the Valleyview Fish and Game Association began lobbying for special regulations on the Little Smoky. They built their case on four points: the wilderness nature of the stream, the uniqueness of its hydrology, the abundance of its aquatic life and the exceptional quality of its fishing.

This group was supported by numerous associations and individuals, including the Fox Creek Fish and Game Association, the Peace Country Fly Fishers, local municipalities, conservation organizations and the influential provincial politician Marvin Moore. In a remarkably short time this coalition was able to convince the Provincial Minister of Forestry, Lands and Wildlife to designate the upper sixty miles of the Little Smoky River as permanent catch-and-release water, beginning in 1989. The no-kill section will be extended farther downstream in 1996 into an area more readily accessible by roads.

The season on the no-kill section of the Little Smoky is from June 16 to October 31 though this may change in the future. There is no bad time to fish this river, as it does not undergo a severe spring runoff. In high-water periods its volume increases and its tea-color darkens slightly, but it is rare for the Little Smoky to be unfishable. It is equally unusual to be on this river when flies aren't hatching and grayling aren't rising. Good bug activity and good fishing last well into October.

What does the future hold for the Peace Country streams? I'm guardedly optimistic. Though the backcountry is being opened up and anglers have access to the fish, it appears that the government is prepared to restrict the harvest to protect the resource. The special attention given the Little Smoky is a good example and a good start.

The Peace Country is now undergoing the most intensive timber harvest anywhere in Alberta, and this will undoubtedly place stress on parts of the fishery. There are, however, signs that the forest industry is willing to work with government

Darryl Smith plays an arctic grayling on the Little Smoky River.
PHOTO BY BOB SCAMMELL

and conservation groups to recognize and protect the sensitive parts of the watershed. One encouraging example is that timber companies and Forestry Canada are now helping to fund fish inventory studies that will identify areas critical to the fishery and that will help in the development of wise timber harvest strategies.

For now the wonderful waters of the Peace system appear to be in good hands. And while the Athabasca system requires rehabilitation, the Peace system requires protection and is beginning to get it. There is a profound difference between the two.

Though there are reasons for optimism here, I still get the feeling that a fine and wonderful resource is balanced on a precipice. Time will tell if we will push it over the edge as we have in the Athabasca Basin, or if we will work together to pull it back to safety. And is it too much of a stretch to view the beautiful trout water in the Peace Country as a reflection of the big picture in Alberta? I think not.

ACCESS AND ACCOMMODATION

Many Peace tributaries are accessible from the Forestry Trunk Road (here called Highway 734), Highway 40 in the Grande Prairie–Grande Cache corridor and from Highway 43 and resource roads for the petroleum and timber industries. Three of the most important of these are the Two Lakes Road southwest of Grande Prairie, the Suncor Road southwest of Valleyview and the Amoco–Bigstone Road northwest of Fox Creek.

The upper portion of the Little Smoky River is accessible from the Huckleberry Tower Road, which connects with Highway 40 east of Grande Cache, or from the Suncor Road. The middle sections are accessible from the Amoco-Bigstone Road.

Campgrounds are scattered throughout the area on the main roads and frequently are situated where they cross the good streams. Motel accommodation is available in the four towns though many hardcore anglers prefer to move about in a self-contained manner, camping, fishing and moving as the streams and fish suggest.

A good map and local directions are a big asset when exploring this country. Maps are available from the Department of Forestry offices in Fox Creek, Valleyview, Grande Cache and Grande Prairie, and from various sporting goods stores. The best map for a general overview of the area is the Alberta Government 1:250,000 Topographic Edition. The 1:50,000 Provincial Resource Base maps are excellent for details of stream access.

HATCH CHART

Date	Hatch	Imitation
June 1 – Sept 15	Caddis	Elk Hair Caddis, size 12 – 18
June 15 – July 10	Brown Willow Fly (stonefly)	Brown Stimulator, size 8 – 12
June 20 – July 15	Pale Morning Dun	Pale Morning Dun Parachute, size 16

July 10 – Aug 10	Western Green Drake	Olive Paradrake, Crystal Green Drake, size 10
Aug 10 – Aug 30	Black Willow Fly (stonefly)	Black Stimulator, size 10, 12
Sept 10 – Oct 5	Blue-winged Olive	Adams, Crystal Blue-winged Olive, size 18, 20

11

The HEALTH *and* WELFARE REPORT

HE REVIEWS on the current health of our stream fisheries are mixed. A wide-angle view would show that
the Oldman, Bow, Red Deer and North Saskatchewan
systems have been diddled with considerably by man, and in
the process we have caught and killed too many native cutthroat and bull trout. We have replaced them with non-native
species that are not as easy to catch, and though opinions vary
on whether this *should* have happened, the fact is it did, and the
fishing in these systems is very good. The backcountry of the
Athabasca watershed was opened up early, allowing us to catch
and kill too many native grayling and bull trout, and the fishing
there has suffered. In the Peace system the native grayling and
bull trout are still around because we haven't been able to get at
them as easily or for as long, and the fishing there is wonderful.

THE GOOD NEWS

I am encouraged that the provincial government is slowly
beginning to realize the economic value of high-quality wild
trout fisheries. People throughout North America are starting

to view Alberta as a place to come to for good trout fishing, and it's a simple fact that while they're here to fish they will spend money. This crass but necessary realization began with the publicity heaped on the Bow River in the 1980s and is continuing with the more recently established reputation of the Crowsnest River.

With this realization came some improvements in trout-stream management. The biologists—the guys and gals with their feet in the water—usually know what our trout streams need, but policy-makers are reluctant to make waves, and change has often been painfully slow. But we do have province-wide no-kill regulations on bull trout today (though we're still waiting for similar rules for arctic grayling) as well as full-time no-kill regulations on the North Ram, Livingstone, upper Smoky and Torrens rivers with more to come. These are steps in the right direction.

Recognition of the importance and desirability of wild fish has been one of Alberta's strong points over the years, and that continues today. Many of our high-profile streams are managed to protect spawning-aged fish, and though this sometimes results in complex angling regulations with seasonal closures and slot-limits, it recognizes the fact that not all streams need the same rules.

In my father's time catch-and-release fishing was something occasionally promoted by people like Ray Bergman in the pages of big outdoor magazines published in New York City (New York City?). Out here in the hinterland the concept was viewed as something of a laughable novelty and maybe even a myth like the one about pike losing their teeth each summer.

In my era anglers began by taking home everything they caught, and later in life some of us were converted to no-kill fishing. The next generation of fly-fishers should be different, for they will be the first to have grown up with the catch-and-release philosophy. This group probably won't view fishing as a way of obtaining food, and even if that is something of a betrayal of the sport's roots, it won't be all bad.

We are fortunate in Alberta to have conservation organizations and individuals who believe passionately in the value of our cold-water fisheries. While an outsider might see this as self-serving, if he looks closely he'll find that though these people like to catch fish, they believe even more deeply in trout streams as symbols of what is good and clean in a world that needs all such virtue it can get. And though the organizations dedicated to these pursuits are not without their problems, they are still the focal points of efforts to keep trout abundant in free-flowing rivers. The leader in Alberta—Trout Unlimited Canada—is an organization that needs the support of all who appreciate Alberta's trout streams.

We have our watchdogs in Alberta, and thankfully many of them are bull terriers who simply won't quit fighting. People like Barry Mitchell, Darryl Smith, Tony Blake and Bob Paget have put far more time and effort into their conservation work than most people put into their jobs.

THE NOT-SO-GOOD NEWS

A bright future for Alberta's trout streams is, however, by no means guaranteed. There are some universal issues and some minor problems specific to individual streams that need our immediate attention.

More of Canada's water is used for irrigation on the prairies than for any other purpose, and the majority of that irrigation takes place in Alberta. In fact eighty percent of all water consumed in Alberta is used for irrigation. And Murphy's Law of Irrigation states that the time of greatest demand will coincide with the time of least supply. Irrigators need the most water in hot, dry summers, when the rivers' flows are at their lowest levels.

The result is concern, particularly in southern Alberta, about how much water will be left between the stream banks. On the Highwood River adherence to instream flow needs established in the early 1990s is leaving more water in the river through the summer, thereby allowing a safe migration of trout and whitefish from the nursery streams down the Bow.

But things are not so simple on the Bow itself. Pressure is being put on the provincial Department of Environmental Protection to establish minimum flow guidelines on the river below Carseland. However, if a suitable minimum flow is established, the department will find that current licenses already allow irrigators to draw the river down below that level. The department clearly faces a dilemma, for not only have they already committed more water to irrigators that they can provide if they are to operate within their own guidelines, but also they need to address new applications requesting more Bow water for irrigation.

Bob Paget lives on the Bow below Carseland, and keeping water in his river has become the focus of his passion. In 1995 he and his wife, Carolynn, established the Southern Alberta River Conservation Foundation, whose first mandate is to ensure that in-stream flow needs in the Bow River are adhered to. In addition the foundation will initiate, assist and fund where necessary the continued gathering of information relating to water quality and environmental concerns on the Bow, Red Deer and Oldman rivers.

Another major concern is the effect of the booming timber industry on our trout streams. Logging is having impact on every watershed in the province, and as we have seen in the Athabasca system, both the removal of the trees and the construction of logging roads cause problems. The logging trails open up the backcountry to growing numbers of people using quads, trikes, ATVs, trail bikes and mountain bikes. The number of people in formerly inaccessible places is going to increase in the future, and the maintenance of our fisheries will depend in part on good enforcement of good regulations. Unfortunately enforcement is perpetually handicapped by the fact that small numbers of officers must try to serve ridiculously large areas.

Another wide-spread concern is the cattle industry. Historically trout and cattle have been a poor mix. When allowed concentrated and constant access to the same part of a stream, cattle rapidly destroy the banks and the riparian vegetation, causing the stream to become wider, shallower and siltier. It happens most easily on creeks with soft stream beds, and the foothill waters of the Red Deer and North Saskatchewan systems have known this problem for decades. But even on gravel-bottomed rivers like the Oldman and the Bow, serious bank deterioration occurs over time.

In recent years discussions between Trout Unlimited, the Alberta Cattle Commission, the Canadian Cattlemen's Association, the Department of Public Lands and the Fisheries Management Division of Alberta's Department of Environmental Protection have begun with the intent to develop and test alternate grazing strategies that can benefit both cattle and trout. These objectives have been supported by all stakeholders, and though it is too early for tangible results, similar plans have been successful in parts of the United States, and we have reason for some optimism here.

Road, town, ski hill, airport and golf course development also take their turns at threatening damage to our stream fisheries. For example, the extensive subdivision and residential development along the Crowsnest River concerns many anglers. Though such development shouldn't have adverse affect on the fish if regulations regarding riparian zones and septic fields are followed, it will have a devastating effect on the quality of experience when fishing there. If the current trend continues the Crowsnest may someday look like the Madison River below Quake Lake in Montana, where the river is a substitute for a street, and houses line both riverbanks for miles.

These problems won't go away and will require knowledgeable, vocal input into the decisions and policies that govern these developments. The best way for an individual to help is to write letters to government representatives, to encourage friends to do the same and to support the organizations that take on the responsibility of addressing such issues.

Beyond these general concerns there are some glaring problems related to current Alberta fishing regulations. For instance, on the Oldman River below Highway 22 the regulations forbid the killing of bull trout yet allow bait-fishing. When caught on bait, fish suffer extremely high mortality rates and catch and release—at least catch and release alive—is not considered compatible with bait-fishing. Saving the streams of the Athabasca system will require drastically reduced limits on rainbow trout and complete no-kill regulations on arctic grayling.

On the Bow River all trout over sixteen inches long are protected downstream of the Highway 22x bridge at the south end of Calgary. Upstream of the bridge, however, the regulations allow bait-fishing and the killing of two fish of any size. The problem occurs in the fall, when large numbers of brown trout migrate into the city to spawn, thereby exposing themselves to the most liberal regulations at the most critical time of their lives. A no-kill, no-bait regulation in the Bow and Elbow rivers through the city in the fall would seem a logical idea.

The Bow continues to face other difficulties related to its location and multipurpose use. Bow River water is needed for drinking, power production, waste-water treatment, irrigation and recreation. In addition the Bow flows through federal, provincial, municipal and Indian reserve land, and continuity of management objectives has never been attained. In addition many people find it perplexing that there is still not a full-time biologist stationed on the most famous trout stream in the country.

The quality of the fishing on the Bow River also is affected in the short term by Calgary. Every time there is a hard rain in the city, the Bow gets very dirty very quickly. The rainwater picks up dirt and debris and carries it directly into the river through the city's storm sewer system, thereby clouding the water and rendering it unfishable until the rain stops.

One interesting idea has the potential to ease this problem sometime in the future. The city has begun a pilot project to test a wetland filter system in a small area of west Calgary. Water collected from storm drains is pumped through a man-made marsh, which filters out sediments before the water reaches the river. If applied on a large scale, this could reduce the volatility of the river and alleviate part of the problem. It will be some years until the viability of this idea is known and even longer until its results will be felt in a big way, but it is intriguing. Similar systems of engineered wetlands have been successful in several regions of the United States.

The Bow River gets dirty easily for a number of reasons

other than rainfall, including pipeline, bridge and residential construction in the city as well as unexpected releases of water from both the Bearspaw and Glenmore dams. Sudden changes in the level or clarity of the water often occur without warning. When this happens at the peak of fishing season, a significant tourist attraction is in essence temporarily shut down without the tour operators (the guides and outfitters) having advance notice. It is a pet concern of mine that the fishability of the Bow below Calgary is not a factor in the way the river is managed.

On the international trout front there is unfortunately some very bad news. In 1994 it was determined that a parasitic infection known as Whirling Disease, which affects mostly immature rainbow trout, was present in Montana's Madison River. The disease caused a ninety percent decline in the population of rainbows in the infected reaches of the river. This disease spreads primarily downstream and is expected to shortly have serious impact on the entire Missouri River watershed. It was formerly thought to exist only in hatchery fish, but it is now confirmed in a number of wild trout fisheries in other Rocky Mountain states, including Colorado and Idaho, as well as in Montana watersheds west of the Continental Divide. There is no known cure for Whirling Disease, and for these fisheries to remain rainbow trout streams, scientists must find or develop a strain of trout resistant to the disease.

The parasite's spores can be moved from one watershed to another by birds, by the transport of fish or fish parts and at least theoretically by wading equipment and boats used by anglers on infected waters. The spores are extremely hardy and are believed to be capable of surviving up to thirty years in dried mud.

The Alberta government's position on Whirling Disease

makes me nervous. Officials say there is no sign of the disease in Alberta (though there have been no comprehensive tests done to find out) and it is unlikely it could be transported over the great distance from Montana to Alberta. Great distance? It takes four hours to drive from the Missouri River to the Crowsnest. Each summer thousands of people fish both Montana and Alberta trout streams. Many of them use boats and virtually all of them use waders. Let's thoroughly investigate this by first testing our hatcheries and then our wild trout for the presence of the disease. We can't afford not to know.

So what of the future of Alberta's trout streams? Though the current state of affairs is quite good in most areas, if the quality of our fishing is to be maintained or even improved we'll have to work as hard as ever to foster a conservative attitude among anglers and a proactive position among government policy-makers in matters of protecting habitat and regulating harvest. Alberta is still one of the best places in the world to fly-fish, but the future is not guaranteed. We can go either way from here.

12

FLY PATTERNS

T HE HATCH CHARTS in chapters six through ten recommend both well-known standard flies and some more recently developed patterns. The recipes for effective, well-known flies like the Adams, Wooly Bugger and Gold Ribbed Hare's Ear are readily available elsewhere, so they will not be described here.

New fly patterns are too often created for the wrong reasons. Rather than filling a niche or serving a need, they are often invented simply to draw acclaim (and sometimes royalties) to the inventor. Here I have tried to choose inventions that still have necessity in their maternal heritage.

The flies that appear here have caught my attention for reasons of effectiveness, durability and originality. A few are my inventions, some are the work of tiers far more creative than I and some are simply new variations on old favorites.

Please consider any and all of these patterns as starting points only. Feel free to change, adapt and alter as inspiration and experience suggest, for like great food recipes, great fly patterns evolve under the direction of numerous creative minds.

DRY FLIES

Crystal Blue-winged Olive

Afternoon hatches of small Baetis *mayflies occur on most Alberta streams in both spring and fall. The best hatches take place in the worst weather, and the fish usually feed on the fall's hatch more readily than the spring's. This imitation partially solves the greatest problem with fishing this hatch: the difficulty in seeing the fly on the water.*

Hook:	Mustad 94840, Tiemco 100 or 101, or Orvis Big Eye, sizes 18 and 20
Tail:	Dun hackle fibers or Microfibetts
Body:	Fine brown-olive dubbing
Wing:	Single post of pearl Crystal Flash
Hackle:	Blue dun, tied parachute style

Stimulator

This fly was devised by Oregon tier Randall Kaufmann in the 1980s and has quickly become a standard throughout the West. By varying colors and sizes you can use it to represent grasshoppers, caddisflies and both types of giant stoneflies.

Hook:	Mustad 94831 or Tiemco 200R, sizes 4 through 16
Tail:	Natural or bleached elk hair
Abdomen:	Orange or yellow Fly Rite, or Antron dubbing
Rear Hackle:	Grizzly or brown, palmered through abdomen

Rib:	Fine gold or copper wire, reverse-wrapped over rear hackle
Wing:	Natural or bleached elk hair
Thorax:	Orange or yellow Fly Rite, or Antron dubbing to contrast abdomen
Front Hackle:	Grizzly or brown dry-fly hackle to contrast rear hackle, palmered through thorax
Head:	Fluorescent orange tying thread

Crystal Green Drake

The Western Green Drake is an important insect on many western streams, including Alberta's North Raven River and most streams in the Oldman drainage. This pattern incorporates the dubbed body and wing of Crystal Flash into the Paradrake style of fly popularized by Mike Lawson of Idaho. With appropriate color changes it can be a good Brown Drake imitation as well.

Hook:	Mustad 94840, Tiemco 100 or equivalent, sizes 10 and 12
Tail:	Several dark moose body hairs
Body:	Moose body hair tied in extended-body fashion, then covered with fine olive dubbing
Rib:	Single strand of olive or gray Crystal Flash, ribbed from hook bend to base of wing
Wing:	Single post of olive or gray Crystal Flash
Hackle:	Grizzly dyed olive, tied parachute style

Quad March Brown

The Quad series of dry flies is the work of St. Albert fly-tier Roman Scharabun. It incorporates a number of proven ideas into one productive pattern. It can be used to imitate any mayfly by simply adjusting the size and colors of the materials.

Hook:	Mustad 94840, Tiemco 100 or equivalent, sizes 12 and 14
Trailing Shuck:	Olive Z-lon
Abdomen:	Single brown turkey biot, wrapped
Thorax:	Brown Antron dubbing
Wing:	Single post of gray turkey body feather
Hackle:	Light blue dun, tied parachute style

Pale Morning Dun Parachute

The Pale Morning Dun is one of our most universal and important mayflies. The parachute type of mayfly imitation is the best I've found for consistently landing upright on the water.

Hook:	Mustad 94840, Tiemco 100 or equivalent, or Orvis Big Eye, size 16
Tail:	Dun hackle fibers or Microfibetts
Body:	Fine, creamy olive dubbing
Wing:	Single post of gray turkey body feather
Hackle:	Blue dun, tied parachute style

Hopper-cator

Mike Guinn has been an animal trainer for Walt Disney and a detective for the Calgary police force. He now guides fly-fishers full time, half the year on the Bow River and half in Costa Rica. His grasshopper pattern is visible, buoyant and effective. Mike likes to tie a second piece of leader tippet into the eye of this fly and hang a small bead head nymph underneath it. Hence the fly is simultaneously a dry fly and an "edible indicator" for the nymph below it.

Hook:	Mustad 9672 or Tiemco 5263, sizes 6 through 10
Tail:	Red bucktail
Body:	Yellow foam, wrapped, with a piece left extending over tail
Rear Hackle:	Undersized brown hackle, palmered over foam
Underwing:	Black moose mane
Overwing:	Natural light elk hair
Front Hackle:	Undersized grizzly and brown, mixed

Nymphs

Pennstone
(weighted)

Golden stoneflies are important bugs in many Alberta streams, and this is my favorite imitation of the nymph. It was devised by Jim Gilson and Dave McMullen to match the nymphs in Penns Creek and other Pennsylvania freestone streams, but it has proved effective elsewhere. This fly is not difficult to tie but is time-consuming. To me it is well worth the effort because it works so well.

Hook:	Mustad 79580, Tiemco 200R or equivalent, sizes 4 through 10
Weight:	.025 or .020 lead wire, wrapped under body
Tails:	Two brown goose biots, tied split
Overbody:	Mottled turkey tail, stiffened with Dave's Flexament
Abdomen:	Yellow or gold Antron, or Hare's Ear Plus dubbing
Rib:	Medium copper wire
Thorax:	Yellow or gold Antron, or Hare's Ear Plus dubbing
Wing Cases:	Mottled turkey tail, folded into three segments (can be same piece used for overbody, or separate piece)
Legs:	Six clumps of medium brown hen saddle hackle, tied in three pairs, De Feo style

Poly Stone Nymph
(weighted)

This is a good imitation of the Pteronarcys *genus of stoneflies— the giant salmonfly. It sinks quickly and presents a good silhouette to the trout.*

Hook:	Mustad 79580, Tiemco 200R or equivalent, sizes 4 through 8
Weight:	.025 lead wire, wrapped under body
Tails:	Two black goose biots, tied split

Abdomen:	Tightly wrapped black or dark brown poly-propylene yarn (often called Phentex)
Rib:	Medium copper wire
Thorax:	Medium brown chenille
Hackle:	Brown or black hackle, palmered through thorax
Wing Case:	Remainder of polypropylene yarn pulled forward over thorax

Bead Head Prince Nymph

The bead head phenomenon struck North America in 1992 and 1993, but the flies were popular in Europe for a long time before that. The Prince Nymph is just one fly to which a brass bead has been added with great success. I have no idea what this fly represents, which is probably why I don't use it much, but it is immensely popular.

Hook:	Mustad 9671, Tiemco 5262 or equivalent, sizes 8 through 14
Tails:	Two brown goose biots, tied split
Body:	Peacock Herl
Rib:	Medium gold oval tinsel
Wings:	Two white goose biots, tied down
Hackle:	Brown hen, tied soft-hackle style
Bead:	Brass, placed over hook shank and positioned at front of fly

Magic Stone

This bead head stonefly nymph is the creation of Calgary tier Glenn Smith. It gets the attention of fish in the Bow and Crowsnest rivers particularly.

Hook:	Mustad 9672, Tiemco 5263 or equivalent, sizes 6 through 10
Tails:	Two brown goose biots, tied split
Overbody:	Medium brown marabou fibers
Abdomen:	Cream or gold rabbit fur dubbing
Rib:	Medium copper wire
Thorax:	Gold Lite Bright dubbing
Wing case:	Remainder of marabou pulled forward over thorax
Hackle:	Brown hen saddle, tied soft-hackle style
Bead:	Brass, placed over hook shank and positioned at front of fly

Hare and Pheasant
(weighted or unweighted)

This is a hybrid with great bloodlines. It was shown to me by former Albertan Bob Vaile, now a New Zealand guide and raconteur. It's perhaps the ultimate "why didn't I think of that" fly.

Hook:	Mustad 9671, Tiemco 5262 or equivalent, sizes 8 through 14

Tail:	Natural brown cock ring-necked pheasant tail fibers
Abdomen:	Natural brown cock ring-necked pheasant tail fibers, wrapped
Rib:	Fine copper wire
Thorax:	Natural brown Hare's Ear Plus, dubbed rough
Wing case:	Pheasant tail fibers pulled forward over thorax
Legs:	Tips of pheasant tail fibers folded back along body

Soft Hackle Hare's Ear
(weighted or unweighted)

The addition of a soft hen hackle to a conventional Gold Ribbed Hare's Ear is the last step in the evolution of a perfect trout fly. It can be tied in many colors, including brown, olive and gold.

Hook:	Mustad 9671, Tiemco 2312 or equivalent, sizes 8 through 14
Tail:	Soft, medium brown hen hackle
Abdomen:	Natural, olive or gold Hare's Ear Plus dubbing
Rib:	Gold oval tinsel (optional)
Thorax:	Natural, olive or gold Hare's Ear Plus, dubbed rough
Wing case:	Mottled turkey segment pulled over thorax
Hackle:	Soft, brown hen hackle

McFlash
(weighted or unweighted)

McFlash is a generic dark nymph with a little sparkle to get the attention of fish. Like many other good flies it uses peacock herl in the body, which trout everywhere seem to love.

Hook:	Mustad 9671, Tiemco 2312 or equivalent, sizes 8 through 14
Tail:	Short clump of soft black hen hackle
Abdomen:	Black rabbit fur or Hare's Ear Plus dubbing
Rib:	Medium copper wire
Thorax:	Peacock herl
Wing case:	Copper Crystal Flash pulled forward over thorax
Legs:	Two or three fibers of wing case material folded back on each side of body

STREAMERS

Geek Leech

This fly was developed by Bow River guides in the late 1980s. A simple fly to tie, it is most effective when fished deep and slow. It can be tied in a variety of colors, including brown, black, olive or wine.

Hook:	Mustad 79580, Tiemco 300 or equivalent, sizes 2 through 10
Tail:	Piece of variegated mohair yarn, combed out,

	or piece of marabou to match body color
Body:	Remainder of mohair yarn, wrapped forward and combed out to form translucent sheath around body
Eyes:	Lead, plain or painted

Clouser Minnow

This is a smallmouth bass fly developed by Pennsylvania angler Bob Clouser that has emigrated to catch dozens of species of fish in fresh- and saltwater throughout the world. The combination of lead eyes and sparse body makes it sink quickly and cast comfortably. It works particularly well when attached to the leader with an open loop knot like a Duncan Loop. Skeptics call it nothing more than a jig for a fly rod. I call it a great idea.

Hook:	Mustad 79580, Tiemco 300 or equivalent, sizes 2 through 8
Overwing:	Sparse brown, black or dark olive bucktail, mixed with pearl Crystal Flash
Underwing:	Sparse white bucktail
Eyes:	Lead, plain, chrome or painted

Note: Fly is tied inverted

Spring Creek Bugger
(also called Lucky Leech)

I wanted a streamer to use in small, clear streams. This one lands unobtrusively yet sinks quickly and has enough bulk and movement to appeal to big trout. It can be tied in a variety of colors, including brown and olive.

Hook:	Mustad 90240, Tiemco 7989 or equivalent, sizes 8 through 12
Tail:	Short clump of fluffy black marabou, mixed with green Crystal Flash
Body:	Black Crystal Chenille or Lite Bright dubbing
Overbody:	Remainder of Crystal Flash pulled forward over body
Eyes:	Brass, tied in at front of hook
Hackle:	Soft, black hen hackle

Crystal Blue-winged Olive

Stimulator

Crystal Green Drake

Quad March Brown

Pale Morning Dun Parachute

Hopper-cator

Pennstone

Poly Stone Nymph

Bead Head Prince Nymph

Magic Stone

Hare and Pheasant

Soft Hackle Hare's Ear

McFlash

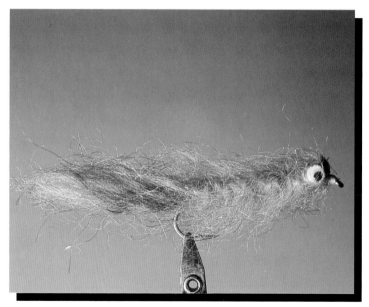

Geek Leech

Clouser Minnow

Spring Creek Bugger

13

The DREAM SEASON

THE NIGHT AIR was sharp with the pungent scent of October. I had closed the fishing season with a Thanksgiving Day float on the Bow, and after feeding the dog and putting my daughter to bed I watched a black-and-white rerun of *Mission Impossible* and then drew a hot bath to ward off the autumn chill. I eased my tired bones into the tub, and through closed eyes wistfully watched another fishing season slip from present to past. As always it was over before I had fished half the places I intended.

I began to drift off, and after a time the drip of the faucet became the gurgle of a trout stream that was overlaid by the stirring of a gentle breeze that became a voice. . . .

"Your mission, should you choose to accept it, is to forgo all trivial activity for the period between April 15 and September 30 and dedicate yourself wholly to fly-fishing. Some restrictions apply. You must fish within the boundaries of the province of Alberta, and you must fish moving water and only moving water."

"Should I choose to accept it? What kind of choice is that?" I heard myself ask. "But who are you?"

"I am the U.A.F.A., the Ultimate and Absolute Fishing

Authority, the one who assigns important angling tasks to qualified individuals."

"And I'm qualified?"

"Unquestionably. No one else has shown the consistently high commitment to irresponsibility that this assignment requires."

I immediately began preparations for my demanding project. I was given a sizable expense account, which was suitably drained obtaining a new drift boat, camping equipment, much new tackle, lots of maps and a big cooler. Friends in Rocky Mountain House, Blairmore and Jasper were called, trips were arranged, schedules planned.

April 15 arrived and I was smiling all the way to the bank— the bank of the Bow. This was going to be great. I tied a Hare's Ear Nymph to a 4x leader, stepped into the water and began to cast. In no time I caught a big brown, then a big rainbow. Things were going just the way I'd hoped they would. I wasn't even catching any whitefish. I always suspected fishing would be better without the nagging interference of a conscience.

My gloating was interrupted by a pain in my toes. The water is cold this early in the season, I thought, as I landed another big rainbow. "Boy, the water is *really* cold," I said aloud after all feeling had left my feet. Then I realized that my waders—those new, expensive waders—were leaking. My feet were wet, my legs were wet, and now, somehow, even my hair and face were wet. . . .

Slowly the babble of the river faded to be replaced with the faint sound of harp music. My vision went blurry for a moment, and when it returned I was staring at the bathroom ceiling and my neck hurt. I climbed out of the icy water, grabbed a towel and drained the tub.

Only a dream, I suppose, but the prospect of such a fishing season is an intriguing fantasy I think about from time to time. And if it *were* to happen, what would I do?

Well, on opening day I would arrange to be on the Bow below Calgary. I'd park at the top of the valley a few miles from town and climb down the hill to the river. The grass would be tired and bent from the stress of six months under snow, and I'd be tired and bent from the stress of six months without fishing. The weather might be bad, but I know the day would be great simply because of what opening days represent. Crocuses would dot the prairie, and I'd be eager to get started.

Working upriver, fishing the choppy slots and depressions along the bank, I might catch some whitefish, a few small rainbows and the occasional brown trout. My target, though, would be a lovely piece of flat water, where I have spent the best dry-fly moments of my life. With luck there would be some cloud cover and the Blue-winged Olives would hatch heavily in the afternoon. Though Bow fish largely disdain this hatch in the spring, if I were patient I might find a good one working, and today one would be enough.

April would be mainly shakedown time, a chance to get the bugs out of new tackle, to make sure enough flies were tied for the project and to plan and scheme for the rest of the season. Most fishing trips would be low-key checks on the condition of various streams punctuated by lunches in strategic country coffee shops. There would be short bouts of nymphing in preparation for the prime months to come.

In early May I would pull my hat down a little tighter and head south to the Crowsnest River west of Pincher Creek. There would still be some spawning rainbows around, and I'd have to be careful not to disturb redds in the gravel. Fish would be eager for a carefully presented Pheasant Tail Nymph, which I'd tell myself they take for a March Brown mayfly.

After a morning of nymphing I'd eat my sandwich at the picnic table overlooking Lundbreck Falls and watch big rainbows from the lower river trying to jump the falls.

After lunch I'd find some March Browns hatching sporadically and maybe a few fish eating them. I'd carefully check a favorite run along some overhanging spruce trees a few miles above Lundbreck. When the sun began to drop behind Turtle Mountain I'd point the truck into the wide valley between the Porcupine Hills and the Livingstone range and head north on Highway 22 for home. Ian Tyson would sing "Springtime in Alberta" as the Rockies turned rose, and I'd look for deer and elk in the meadows near the road. A glance at the Oldman River from the Waldron bridge would remind me of a date we had for later in the summer.

With some of the winter rust now off and the fishing season truly rolling, I would dedicate the next couple of months to some serious hatch-chasing. Many of our best and most reliable insect hatches occur between early May and mid-July, so my schedule would be carefully planned to try to meet as many of them as possible. This bug fixation brings dilemmas, though, and sometime in May I'd face the first one. It would be time to start directing some attention to the waters of the West Country—that beautiful area of rolling hills, mixed forest and brown trout between the towns of Cochrane and Rocky Mountain House. A few days on these streams looking for March Browns would be necessary to avoid shirking my delicious responsibility. The fish would be relatively few, but they would be beautiful, orange-spotted brown trout, and if things went well, a couple of them might be big.

But it also would be hard to ignore a river as special as the Bow when something important begins to happen. Mid-May brings the first good hatches of caddisflies on the reaches below Calgary. These are not the caddis that pour out of the willows every evening later in the summer, but are rather a more civilized group, emerging on bright, sunny afternoons. My wife, Lynda, and I would float from Policeman's Landing to McKinnon Flats, looking for rising fish. When we found them they would likely be a little naive and quite easy to catch. It wouldn't bother me to take advantage of this though, because I know these same fish will get even in September. We would catch mostly brown trout now because many rainbows are up spawning in the Highwood system. Families of Canada geese would be everywhere on the river, sometimes annoying impatient fly-fishers by nonchalantly chugging their way through pods of rising fish.

The Crowsnest River would also require further attention in late May for what many anglers consider to be the most important event of its season. It is then that the giant black stonefly nymphs (called salmonflies) begin their migration from midriver to the banks in preparation for hatching. The river level might begin to rise with melting snow brought down by the hot sun, but with eighteen inches or more of visibility in the water, the fishing with big black nymphs could be spectacular. This is a time for full-contact fly-fishing requiring aggressive wading in fast, bouldery water and size 4 or 6 heavily weighted nymphs on 2x leaders. This is fly-fishing without finesse, and it is wonderfully entertaining. The casting is clumsy and ugly, and the fish anything but. Below Lundbreck Falls is some of the best stonefly water on the continent, and the rainbows that roar off into my backing might average close to eighteen inches through this period.

By early June the streams of the Oldman and Bow systems would be in full runoff, and I would again return to the West Country and in particular to the area around Caroline.

That nasty little spring creek, the North Raven River, would be calling my name. The fishing here is *all* finesse, and this little stream would quickly drain me of whatever cockiness I had acquired on the Crow. Mid-June here delivers Pale Morning Dun mayflies in the mornings, Green Drakes in the afternoons and giant Brown Drakes late in the evening. Back at the bridge after dark I would undoubtedly run into other North Raven Regulars—Don Andersen, Barry Mitchell or Bob Scammell—who would regale me with stories of fish just a little bigger than mine.

By late June the Bow would be back in shape, and both caddis and Pale Morning Duns would be hatching daily. A few overnight float trips would be essential with campsites carefully chosen to provide late evening binges of dry-fly fishing. These are the longest days of the year, when it doesn't get dark until 10:30 P.M., but the fish seem to feed infinitely on into the night. Camping on the river would allow me the luxury of fishing as late as I wanted before simply collapsing into a sleeping bag.

After dark the fishing on the Bow takes on a macabre tone as you cast into the darkness, listen for a slurp and then strike to see if it was your fly the fish ate. Fighting a fish you cannot see is likewise an eerie experience. You don't know how big he is until it's all over and you aim the flashlight into the landing net to discover a brown shape bigger than you would have thought to hope for.

Through these long summer days I'd be sharing the big river with many foreign visitors, some here for the first time, some on their annual visit to one of North America's most celebrated trout streams.

In July the Bow would get most of my attention, but I would keep things in perspective with side trips to small streams like the Carbondale River, Cataract Creek or the Sheep River with my fishing partner and daughter, Deanna. But sooner than I realize, half the summer would be over and an extended road trip north would be in order.

August is prime time in the high country of the North Saskatchewan system, and my first stop would be on the North Ram River, west of Rocky Mountain House, where the west-slope cutthroats would chew on my big dry flies. By stationing myself at the campground south of Nordegg, I could also fish Shunda Creek for brown trout. After a few days here I'd continue north on the Forestry Trunk Road to freelance my way through less familiar country. My plan would be to try more cutthroat waters, especially the Blackstone and Cardinal rivers, but I might talk myself into a side trip west on Highway 11 to fish the Bighorn and the Cline.

Continuing north on Highway 40 across the upper Brazeau River, I'd enter the Athabasca watershed. At Hinton, there would be another decision to make. One option would be to shift east and fish the McLeod River near Edson for rainbows and grayling. From there I could continue north to try for grayling in the Whitecourt and Swan Hills region before making a three-day excursion to the best of our grayling streams, the Little Smoky River.

Another option from Hinton would be to continue north on Highway 40 and fish the Berland and Wildhay rivers before getting serious about bull trout on the Muskeg River near Grande Cache. Better still, I could stay another week and do it all.

By early September I'd be winding my way back south and would take a detour into Jasper National Park. Presuming the budget was still solvent, I'd arrange for a packhorse trip up the Snake Indian River near the north boundary of the park for bull trout. Ever since I was a kid spending summers in Jasper with my parents, I've been enchanted by that river's name, and this would be a chance to compare reality with my imagination.

After this trip my legs and rear end would be sore, so I'd stay in Jasper for a couple of more days to heal and also fish one of the most unique places in the world. It's actually a lake—that is, except in late summer when it turns into a river. When Medicine Lake has receded until all that's left is the Maligne River flowing through the lake bed, the entire population of fish is concentrated in the river channel, and the fishing for big, strong rainbows is excellent.

Wait a minute. It's late September already. What about the rest of the places on my list—places like the Highwood River, Dogpound Creek, the upper Oldman (and the lower Oldman), the Castle River, the Kakwa and the Waterton? I'd have to work in some hopper fishing on the Bow and the Blue-winged Olives on the Crowsnest. I'd want to float the Bow above Canmore as well as below Carseland. I thought I could do it all, but there wouldn't be time to do half of it. Can I revise the terms of my contract? I want a long-term deal. Instead of one season, how about one lifetime? That's what it would take.

USEFUL
FURTHER
READING

BOOKS OF LOCAL IMPORTANCE

McLennan, Jim. *Blue Ribbon Bow.* Edmonton: Lone Pine
  Publishing, 1987.
  *An examination of the Bow River as a trout fishery and as an
  important river.*

Norman, J. Gregg, ed. *Fish & Tell & Go To Hell: Alberta Fly-
  fishing Wisdom.* Calgary: Dirtwater Publications, 1989.
  A collection with chapters by noted Alberta fly-fishing writers.

Scammell, Bob. *The Outside Story.* Edmonton/Scarborough:
  Reidmore/Fleet, 1982.
  *A collection of outdoor essays relating to hunting and fishing in
  Alberta.*

Scammell, Bob. *The Phenological Fly: A Guide to Meeting and
  Matching the Super Hatches of the West.* Red Deer: Johnson
  Gorman Publishers, 1995.
  *A pocket-sized guide to the correlation between the hatch times
  of aquatic insects the bloom times of streamside wild flowers.*

VIDEOS OF LOCAL IMPORTANCE

Bow River Adventure. With Gary Boger. Gary Borger's Great
   Waters Series. Borger Films Ltd., 1987.
   A good tape focusing on the dry-fly methods needed on this river.

Fishing Southern Alberta Trout Streams. With Jim McLennan.
   Angling Fantasies, 1992.
   *Samples of streams and instruction of methods for the Bow,
   Crowsnest and North Raven rivers.*

Fly Fishing Alberta Canada's Bow River. With Lefty Kreh.
   Outdoor Safari International Video, n.d.
   Lefty fishes the Bow with Barry White.

Fly Fishing Alberta's Chinook Country. With Vic Bergman. Fly
   Fishing International Inc., n.d.
   *Showcases four rivers and numerous lakes in southwestern
   Alberta.*

Trout – Tying and Fishing Effective Trout Flies. With Vic
   Bergman. Randy Tomiuk Productions, 1993.
   *A fly-tying tape with interludes of Alberta lake and stream
   fishing.*

BOOKS OF GENERAL IMPORTANCE

Hafele, Rick, and Dave Hughes. *The Complete Book of Western
   Hatches.* Portland: Frank Amato Publications, 1981.
   *An examination of the most important western bugs and fly
   patterns to imitate them.*

Rosenbauer, Tom. *The Orvis Fly-fishing Guide.* New York: Nick
  Lyons Books, 1984.
  A good, basic instructional book.

Schwiebert, Ernest. *Trout.* New York: Clark, Irwin & Company,
  1978.
  *A huge, two volume work containing more than you'll ever
  want to ask about trout and fly-fishing for them.*

Swisher, Doug and Carl Richards. *Selective Trout: A Dramati-
  cally New and Scientific Approach to Trout Fishing on Eastern
  and Western Rivers.* New York: Crown, 1971.
  One of the first "bug books" of the new era.

Videos of General Importance

Basic Fly Casting. With Doug Swisher. Mastery Learning System,
  n.d.
  A very good casting tape.

Fly Fishing for Trout. With Gary Borger. Sportman's Video
  Collection, n.d.
  A good, basic instructional tape.

Nymphing. With Gary Borger. Borger Films Ltd., 1982.
  The first instructional fly-fishing tape and still one of the best.

Strategies for Selective Trout. With Doug Swisher. Mastery
  Learning System, n.d.
  One of the best teachers teaching intermediate-level techniques.

Groups, Organizations and Clubs

Groups and Organizations

Trout Unlimited Canada
P.O. Box 6270, Station D
Calgary, Alberta
T2P 2C8

The Bow River Foundation
2938 – 11 Street N.E.
Calgary, Alberta
T2E 7L7

Southern Alberta River Conservation Foundation
c/o Box 6270, Station D
Calgary, Alberta
T2P 2C8

Clubs

There are fly-fishing clubs in most Alberta cities as well as in some smaller centers. In addition, there are numerous active chapters of Trout Unlimited Canada scattered around the province. Information on clubs and Trout Unlimited Canada chapters can usually be obtained from fly and tackle shops in their area, and most of the shops can be found advertising in the *Alberta Fishing Guide* each year.

Here is a list of clubs I am aware of:

Calgary Hook and Hackle Club
P.O. Box 6949, Station D
Calgary, Alberta
T2P 2G2

Brooks Fly Fishing Club
c/o Box 1534
Brooks, Alberta
T1R 1C4

Edmonton Trout Fishing Club
c/o 10125 – 97 Avenue
Edmonton, Alberta
T5K 0B3

Peace Country Fly Fishers
c/o 9840 – 81 Avenue
Grande Prairie, Alberta
T8V 3T1

Sheep River Fly Fishing Club
c/o 54 Lock Cresent
Okotoks, Alberta
TOL IT2

About the Author

Jim McLennan is a native Albertan born in Edmonton in 1953. He was one of the first fly-fishing guides on the Bow River, working from 1976 – 1982. In 1982 he became a partner in Country Pleasures, a fly-fishing store in Calgary.

His first magazine article was published in 1979, and his work continues to appear frequently in major Canadian and international publications, including *Fly Fisherman, Outdoor Canada* and *Gray's Sporting Journal*. He is currently fly-fishing columnist for *Real Outdoors* magazine. His writing also has appeared in a number of outdoor anthologies, including *Fish & Tell & Go To Hell*.

Jim's first book, *Blue Ribbon Bow*, is the definitive work on Alberta's Bow River and was honored as Canada's Outdoor Book of the Year in 1987. In 1992 he was featured in a sixty-minute video, *Fishing Southern Alberta Trout Streams*.

Jim has been teaching fly-fishing since 1976 and has been a featured speaker for fly-fishing clubs and conservation organizations throughout North America, including the 1993 World Fly Fishing Championships, where he spoke at a conservation symposium. In 1988 he was presented with the Greg Clark Award for contributions to the arts of fly-fishing by the prestigious Izaak Walton Fly Fishing Club of Toronto.

Jim McLennan is an active member of Trout Unlimited Canada and was a founding director of both the Edmonton and Calgary chapters of the organization. He lives with his wife and daughter in Okotoks, Alberta.